EMINENT ELIZABETHANS

A. L. Rowse

D0486722

The University of Georgia Press
Athens

First edition 1983
Reprinted 1983

Published in the USA by
THE UNIVERSITY OF GEORGIA PRESS
Athens, Georgia 30602

ISBN 0-8203-0649-5

Library of Congress Cataloging in Publication Data

Rowse, A. L. (Alfred Leslie), 1903–
Eminent Elizabethans.

Includes bibliographical references and index.
1. Great Britain—History—Elizabeth, 1558–1603—
Biography. 2. Great Britain—Biography. I. Title.
DA358.A1R59 1983   942.05'5'0922 [B]   82-13484
ISBN 0-8203-0649-5

Printed in Hong Kong

To
Jacqueline Kennedy Onassis
historic figure
for her love of history

Contents

List of Plates

Preface

It is many years since I first entertained the hope of following up Lytton Strachey's *Eminent Victorians* with an *Eminent Elizabethans*. In the innocence of my younger years I thought it would provide a contrast, work out more heroically, certainly less cynically, than that work in which Strachey sat rather loosely to historical truth. He was more concerned to caricature, and raise a laugh.

The true historian is concerned only to get at the truth. My studies of famous Elizabethans are in no sense caricatures, though they come out less heroically than the ardour of youth expected.

My chief obligation is in regard to the not unheroic figure of Bess of Hardwick. Her successor there, the late Evelyn, Duchess of Devonshire, most hospitably entertained me at Hardwick during three or four summers, and helped me enormously by having Bess's papers and household books brought over from Chatsworth for me to study – so that that portrait is largely based on research into original manuscripts. My great regret is that I have been so long in producing the result that my kind hostess is no longer here to see the work in which she took so much interest.

The study of Father Parsons was given, in shortened form, as one of the annual lectures for Lambeth Palace Library. Some years ago the then Director of the Folger Shakespeare Library, Washington, D.C., urged me to write an account of the Elizabethan Earl of Oxford: here it is at last. In the portrait of Sir John Harington I have been able to identify two of the

leading characters in his Epigrams, who appear under the names
of Paulus and Faustus – and thus add something new.

I am greatly indebted to Professor Jack Simmons for his
kindly and critical scrutiny of my text.

A. L. ROWSE

1

Bess of Hardwick:
Builder and Dynast

I

ESS of Hardwick was the most remarkable woman in Elizabethan England, of chief historic interest, after the two Queens, Elizabeth I and Mary Queen of Scots, with both of whom she was intimately acquainted over years. She was the grandest woman builder England has ever known, having built the new Hardwick Hall – loveliest of Elizabethan houses – as well as largely rebuilt the old Hall there; she also built the contemporary Chatsworth, a splendid house which later dukes of Devonshire replaced with their present palace. Only her friend Lord Burghley surpassed her in the scale of his building – as he said of himself, 'never out of bricks and mortar'. The same might be said of her.

She was a constructive, creative woman on the grand scale, and this applied even more to her family, for whom these grand houses were intended. It hardly needs saying – though it is a clue to her – that she was a woman of immense business ability, practical, realist, not to say materialist. There went with this, besides shrewd calculating judgment, a forward-planning imagination. Though careful and acquisitive, she was also generous – again on a large scale. Nor was she at all cold-hearted – warm-hearted rather, though her affections were strongly concentrated upon her family. She planned for them and built them up: thus she became the ancestress of three, if not four, dukedoms. Not bad going for the daughter of a small impoverished Derbyshire squire. It brings home to one that the Elizabethan age was one for *la carrière ouverte aux talents* – look at Drake, or Ralegh, or William Shakespeare! In her case, as usual with women, her achievement was brought about along the royal road of matrimony, and by means of it.

Perhaps the most decisive mark of her achievement is that, like the two Queens, she remains alive as a figure of folklore to this day.

Elizabeth Hardwick, born in the early 1520s, was a daughter of John Hardwick and his wife, Elizabeth Leake, small Derbyshire gentry on a par with their neighbours, the Leches of Chatsworth, Knivetons of Marcaston, Foljambes and such. The family was of a good stock, going back to the fourteenth century on their estate of some four or five hundred acres of fair land, arable and pasture, in the parish of Ault Hucknall on the north-east border of the county looking over into Nottinghamshire. John was some forty years when he died, leaving a family of small children to provide for – his son and heir a child, and four daughters to whom he was able to leave only a mere pittance of 40 marks each. Many yeomen were able to leave their daughters a better dowry than that; it offered poor prospects for matrimony.

John Hardwick did his best to protect his child-heir from the predations of wardship, but in vain: it led only to disputes which further impoverished the family. His widow shortly re-married to protect herself and her children – a younger son of the Leches of Chatsworth, who was not much better off. Their only advantage was that they were gentry of good family, armigerous and autochthonous, and so could marry within their class.

An early marriage had been arranged for Bess with the youthful son and heir of a neighbouring squire, Robert Barlow[1] of Great Barlow near Chesterfield, their market town. The advantage of this match was that, as usual with a marriage settlement, a prospective widow got one-third of the income of the estate, which kept that much out of the maw of the Court of Wards if the heir died when under age. This happened after a

year or so of marriage, and Bess succeeded to an income of
£8.15s. a year. It was a very small beginning; but even that led,
in the Elizabethan manner, to legal challenges and further disputes. Bess was early inured to struggle and the hard facts of
life; but she was made of Derbyshire grit, independent-spirited
and well able to look after herself. Her later letters – she was
sufficiently educated, better than usual with girls at the time –
show her to have been forthright of speech. She would have
spoken with a Derbyshire accent: Elizabethans spoke with the
accent of their native countryside – Sir Walter Ralegh, for
instance, 'spake broad Devonshire to his dying day'.

As a girl Bess was taken under the wing of a connexion of the
family, Lady Zouche: this gave her an acquaintance with the
ways of London life and an opportunity to meet people from an
altogether wider circle, nearer the Court, 'the world, the power
and the glory' of Tudor life. Thus, about three years after her
youthful husband's death, she met Sir William Cavendish. He
was a Suffolk man, his elder brother, George, much better
known to us for a charming Tudor biography, that of Cardinal
Wolsey of whom George Cavendish was the devoted attendant.

Sir William was over forty, already twice married when he
wedded Bess in August 1547, at the somewhat improbable hour
of two in the morning, at Bradgate, the house of which something remains, on the edge of Charnwood Forest. This was the
home of the Grey family, of which Lady Jane Grey was the
daughter, her father to become Duke of Suffolk and to lose his
head (and his daughter's) under Queen Mary. The Greys
became patrons and friends of the Cavendish couple and
brought them their chief acquaintance at Court.

Sir William's fortune had been made by the dissolution of the
monasteries; as a commissioner and official of the Court of
Augmentations he had picked up desirable properties, some
around London of the Abbey of St Albans, Lilleshall Abbey in
Shropshire, and as far afield as Cardigan. The opportunity fell
to buy Chatsworth; Bess, who knew every acre in that home
territory, persuaded him to sell off outlying properties to concentrate everything in her native Derbyshire. Sir William was
now Treasurer of the Chamber, with considerable Crown

funds on his hands which he could use – in the traditional manner which lasted up to the late eighteenth century – for his own purposes. He proceeded to use them to extend their holdings in and around Chatsworth, until at his demise he was in debt to the Crown for the immense sum of over £5200 unaccounted for. This was the age when the going was good for the foundation of families to become historic, Cecils and Bacons, Russells and Cavendishes.

The couple produced a family of six healthy children who survived, three sons and three daughters; and we can see Bess's progress into grand society in the godparents recruited for their christening. For their son and heir, Henry, no less a person than the Princess Elizabeth, along with the future Dukes of Northumberland and Suffolk. For William, the second son, Lord Treasurer Paulet, to become Marquess of Winchester, the Marchioness of Northampton, and the Earl of Pembroke. All these were leading Protestants around the young Edward VI. The boy's death led to an about-turn with Catholic Mary's accession and an awkward pass for prominent Edwardians. Bess and Sir William protected their flanks at the christening of the third son, Charles, with Queen Mary and Lord Chancellor Gardiner, Bishop of Winchester, as godparents, along with their old friend the Duke of Suffolk. When he and his daughter were executed, it was a brave piece of loyalty to select Lady Catherine Grey as godparent to a daughter; but it is fair to say that loyalty was characteristic of Bess, and her association with this lady was later to bring her imprisonment in the Tower.

Meanwhile, repairs were to be done at Chatsworth which was in a deplorable state, and for the first time we hear Bess's authentic voice in the directions she sent down. 'Cause the floor in my bedchamber to be made even, either with plaster, clay or lime. . . . Let the brewer make beer for me forthwith for my own drinking and your master . . . if I lack either good beer or charcoal or wood, I will blame nobody so much as I will do you.' The voice is of a Derbyshire directness, crisp and practical. Her favourite Jane was looking after the place, but 'I hear that my sister Jane cannot have things that is needful for her to have amongst you. . . . Like as I would not have a superfluity or waste of anything, so likewise would I have her to have that which is needful or necessary. At my homecoming I shall know more and then I will think as I shall have cause.'

Chatsworth was to be their home, but an entirely new house on the grand scale was envisaged to keep up with such friends as Sir John Thynne, building at Longleat. Sir William wrote to him asking for the loan of his 'cunning plasterer, which hath in your hall made divers pendants and other pretty things'. Representations of the new house show a traditional mansion extending on either side of a fine gateway – as at Coughton or Burghley today; on each side were angular projections, the façade finishing with a turret at either end. Quantities of furnishings were sent down, but the hall was not finished until a dozen years after Sir William's death. Progress was held up for years by his large indebtedness to the Crown and by the various happenings to Bess in the interval.

Sir William died in October 1557, and in August 1559 Bess married Sir William St Loe: a proper match, for St Loe was another of the Edwardian circle into which Bess had graduated and was moreover a trusted personal attendant of the new Queen Elizabeth, her Captain of the Guard. This was the foundation of Bess's life-long close association with the Queen – with its ups and downs – for the new Lady St Loe became a lady-in-waiting. The marriage was a love match, at least on Sir William's part, and once more the handsome red-head gave satisfaction: 'my own, more dearer to me than I am to myself', he would write; or, 'thine who is wholly and only thine, yea, for all time while life lasteth'.

St Loe was well off, with lands in Gloucestershire and Somerset which he was free to dispose of. His younger brother was a bad lot, and Sir William chose to dispose of them to Bess. There is no evidence that she put any pressure upon him to do so; for St Loe's mother stood a good friend to Bess when the brother tried all he could to harm her and her husband. When an apparent attempt to poison them failed, he resorted to a group acquainted with the arts of astrology and sorcery – all very Elizabethan. One of these was Francis Cox, from whom Simon Forman learned in early days and with whom he tangled;[2]

another was Hugh Draper of Bristol, who executed the finest of prisoners' monuments in the Tower, an elaborate astronomical clock with the signs of the zodiac: 'Hew Draper of Brystow made this spheer the 30 daye of Maye anno 1562. Close prisoner 8 monethes 32 wekes 224 dayes 5376 houres.'[3]

Old Lady St Loe's prayer – 'as they have little grace, so God send them little power to do my son St Loe and you any hurt' – was answered: nothing untoward happened to Sir William and his treasure. His goodness to her and her children continued to manifest itself: he arranged for the elder boys, Henry and William, to go to Eton; he provided a dowry for one of the girls; in the end he settled for Cavendish's debt to the Crown with an outright payment of £1000. It can only be said that the Cavendishes had done extremely well out of that: less than one-fifth of the debt in cash while they remained in possession of Chatsworth and the lands they had added to it.

Meanwhile, Bess was in serious trouble through her loyalty to the Greys. Lady Catherine Grey contracted a secret marriage with Edward Seymour: a grave offence, for she was of the blood royal with a near claim to the throne, and Seymour was the son of Protector Somerset who had ruled the land for his nephew, Edward VI. When she came near her time of bearing a child, she confided her plight to Bess, who knew very well what it would portend, and 'fell into great weeping, saying that she was very sorry that she had so done without the consent and knowledge of the Queen'. Bess could have cleared herself by going straight to the Queen and informing against the girl – which was what Lord Robert Dudley immediately did when Lady Catherine resorted to him for help. The fact that Bess did not peach on the poor daughter of the Greys who had been her friends meant that she was held guilty, in Tudor terms, of connivance in Lady Catherine's guilt. All three were dispatched to the Tower, the now legally separated couple and Bess, who remained there for some thirteen weeks – very unfairly as it seems to a modern judgment.

This mishap did not prevent Bess, while there, from using the offices of the Lieutenant of the Tower to fix the terms of a dowry for her step-daughter Anne – Sir William's child by a previous wife – with a marriage in view. St Loe came up hand-somely with 1000 marks: very obliging – the Cavendishes were doing well out of him. On Bess's release from the Tower in 1562 she was able to arrange a marriage for her eldest daughter, Frances, with the heir of the Nottinghamshire Pierreponts, from whom the Dukes of Kingston were to be descended. When Sir William St Loe died in 1565 he did better still for Bess, for she succeeded to his West Country lands as her own personal property. Thus she was independently well endowed, apart from her life-interest in the Barlow and Cavendish estates, her regular widow's thirds.

For another couple of years Bess did not marry again, though rumours of several possible candidates for so eligible a widow circulated at Court. So also did a scandal put about by the tutor of her younger children, one Henry Jackson – and a Fellow of Merton to boot – which reached the ears of the Queen, who referred it to be dealt with by the Archbishop of Canterbury and the Court of High Commission. Unfortunately these records have disappeared, but this was the court that dealt with defamation and libel, often of a sexual nature. Not a breath of such scandal was otherwise uttered against Bess, and Jackson was to be chastised, corporally if necessary, 'for spreading slan-der against Lady St Loe, who has long served with credit in our Court'. Thus the Queen, who always held Bess in respect, in spite of *contretemps*.

She would have been a lady of the Privy Chamber, the family growing up healthily at Chatsworth, which was gradually being furnished on a sumptuous scale. Loads of tapestries went down, grand bedsteads, table carpets and quilts, curtains of red mockado, counterpanes and coverings for chairs of bright col-ours the Elizabethans loved – stuffs of such quality that some remain after centuries, faded to the subdued shades we prefer. Bess was a rich woman, with an independent income from her lands, and – though still carrying her quota of debt in the Elizabethan manner – possessing quantities of plate and jewelry.

By 1567 she was ready to consent to the grandest possible match, with George, 6th Earl of Shrewsbury. Shrewsbury was the head of the Talbot clan, descended from the famous 1st Earl, 'brave Talbot, the terror of the French', as Nashe wrote of William Shakespeare's bringing him alive on the stage again, which made the success of the First Part of *Henry VI*. Shrewsbury was the prime potentate of the northern Midlands, 'brave Talbot' having married the heiress of the large fee of Hallamshire with its centre at Sheffield. An earlier ancestor had married the heiress of rose-red Goodrich Castle on the Wye. The Talbots had been always loyal to the Lancastrian royal house and their successors, the Tudors; and had done extremely well from the dissolution of the monasteries – hence Welbeck Abbey, and they got Shrewsbury and Rufford Abbeys, Tutbury Priory and others lying near their estates. These were vast, and their houses included Sheffield Castle and Manor, Tutbury Castle, splendid Wingfield Manor, of which much remains though a ruin, and Worksop, where the Earl was to erect a towering mansion on its hill.

The Earl was about the same age as Bess and, like her, had by his previous marriage a family of three sons and three daughters. Once more the match was one of love on the husband's side; 'if I should judge of time,' wrote the besotted Earl to his 'dear nun', 'methinks time longer since my coming hither without you, my only joy, than I did since I married you: such is faithful affection, which I have never tasted so deeply of before'. Or again, 'as the pen writes so the heart thinks that, of all earthly joys that hath happened unto me, I thank God chiefest for you: for with you I have all joy and contentation of mind, and without you death is more pleasant to me than life if I thought I should be long from you'. We shall see how that worked out; however, once more Bess was giving every satisfaction as a wife.

A regular dynastic structure was formed by two marriages between their children. The Earl's son and heir, Francis, was already married but had no children; so the second son, Gilbert, who ultimately succeeded to the earldom, was married to Bess's daughter, Mary. The Cavendish heir, Henry, was married to the Earl's daughter, Grace Talbot.

These marriage settlements were complicated and eventually led to a mass of trouble. On the Earl's death Bess would get her regular widow's third of his large revenues – by that she would then receive altogether four lots of widow's thirds from her four husbands, and be rich indeed. Meanwhile, the husband would enjoy the revenues from her unsettled estates – but the Cavendish estate would come to the heir, Henry, in 1571. It is a mistake to found a business arrangement on love, as the Earl was to discover; for he bound himself to make the enormous cash settlements of £20,000 each on Bess's younger sons, William and Charles. There was an element of chance in this, for one or other might die in his minority before the cash became due; but the Cavendish children were healthy and survived. When the time approached the Earl – who had had to pay out immense marriage settlements for his own children – could not meet the demand, and was glad in 1572 to remit his claims on the Cavendish estate for some £550 a year. It all led to trouble, but it was not the only strain upon which the marriage came to shipwreck, and the Earl's love turned to hatred.

Towards the end of 1568 he was given the charge of Mary Queen of Scots – a charge of the greatest trust of any subject, as Queen Elizabeth did not fail to emphasise, and of conspicuous honour, as the Earl was the first to appreciate. Whatever the inconveniences and the strain, he would not give it up until virtually forced to. Long before then Bess wanted him to resign: neither of them could have foreseen what a prolonged burden it would prove. For, at the beginning, Elizabeth was inclined to restore Mary, upon strict conditions. This foundered upon the absolute refusal of the great majority of the Scottish nobles to have her back again at any price. When this became obvious Mary tried to force the issue, by maintaining her own party in Scotland, and in England entering upon the conspiracy to marry Norfolk (once the Pope had freed her from Bothwell – a Protestant marriage!), supported by foreign aid – which would have meant the dethronement of Elizabeth. One consequence was Norfolk's condemnation to death – which Shrewsbury presided over as Lord High Steward 'with weeping tears'. Another was that henceforth Elizabeth had no further intention of helping Mary and watched her every move like a cat a mouse.

Shrewsbury was the obvious person to undertake the peril-

ous charge. He was a convinced Protestant who could be
trusted; so was Bess – neither would succumb to any of Mary's
French wiles, religious or otherwise. The Earl had a number of
large houses around which Mary and her retainers, some sixty
in number, could be moved for the necessary cleansing and
airing of the houses (always a problem, and Mary was for ever
complaining). The Shrewsbury estates were as deep inland as
could be: it would never have done to place her anywhere near
the coast – the Earl of Derby, for example, was thus out of the
question and the family was largely Catholic anyway, Sir
William Stanley ultimately a traitor.

Mary's confinement varied in strictness with the threat that
she posed: at times of crisis and at any sign of attempt at escape
the watch upon her was doubled, the numbers of the guard
increased. But usually Mary was able to take the air, often
hunting in the neighbouring woods, in sufficient company; and
at least half-a-dozen times Mary was permitted to stay at
Buxton, to take the waters and the baths, where she was put up
in the Earl's convenient mansion. Indoors, in the first years, she
saw much of Bess, in whose discretion Elizabeth had confidence
and was always willing for Mary to have her company rather
than that of 'meaner persons'. The two ladies did a lot of
needlework and embroidery together, a considerable number
of specimens of which remain at Hardwick, Oxburgh Hall
and elsewhere. This must have served to occupy part of Mary's
working mind and detract from the amount of time she had for
political intrigue.

A main source of trouble was financial. Shrewsbury was
allowed £52 a week to support Mary's regal charges. She had a
large revenue from France, much of which went on supporting
her faction in Scotland; she was extravagant in the Stuart manner, and her little Court – for she was always treated as the
queen she was, if dethroned – was the resort of Scots supporters, messengers, French and other envoys. It was not only a
full-time job keeping watch, but a drain upon Shrewsbury's
own resources – and he was a careful man (some thought
mean); for all his large revenues his outgoings were always
larger. He minded this very much. Bess herself has never been

given credit for her contribution to the difficult joint assignment; used as she was to the ways and intrigues of Courts, the
experience added a further dimension to her education.

Some evidence of this may be seen in the intrigue upon which
she entered in 1574; for, though it was a matrimonial one of
familiar pattern, it had reverberating repercussions. The target
was no less a person than the murdered Darnley's brother,
Charles Lennox, upon whom devolved Darnley's claims and
who shared of course his Stuart and Tudor blood. The marriages of persons of royal blood were matters of state, because
of their proximity to the succession to the throne. Bess had one
as yet unmarried daughter, and she, with two other designing
matrons – the young man's mother, Margaret Countess of Lennox, and Catherine Duchess of Suffolk – decided to marry up
the promising young couple, Elizabeth Cavendish and Charles
Lennox.

On a private visit to secluded Rufford Abbey they were wedded and bedded, without a word either to the Queen – who
would certainly have countermanded it – or to Shrewsbury.
The marriage had all kinds of consequences, foreseen and
unforeseen. Anyone could see the ambition on Bess's side – the
near prospect of her progeny, that of a Derbyshire squire's
daughter, succeeding to the thrones of England and Scotland.
It was not a remote prospect either: Charles Lennox was next
in line to James VI, as yet unmarried. Before Lennox's death
the marriage produced the little Arbella Stuart, whose life was
clouded by her proximity to the throne. This was to turn Mary
Stuart's friendship with Bess into hostility, particularly after
Bess made the mistake of uttering her hopes for her grandchild
to what the Queen of Scots regarded as her right.

A seed of mistrust was also sown between Bess and her husband, who placed above all things his fidelity to his own Queen.
For the present he was under the necessity of defending his
wife, though one can hear the embarrassment in his accents: 'the
young man fell into liking with my wife's daughter . . . and
such liking was between them as my wife tells me she makes no
doubt of a match'. The Earl was the first person to tell the
Queen: the affair had been 'dealt in suddenly and without my

knowledge'. As Shrewsbury wrote to Burghley, it was not the marriage in itself that created so much ado and roused such hostility, 'it is a greater matter, which I leave to conjecture, not doubting your lordship hath foreseen it'. No doubt he meant the succession to the throne.

Elizabeth sent old Lady Lennox – who, as Henry VII's granddaughter, has a fine tomb in his chapel in Westminster Abbey – to the Tower. Bess seems to have got away with it – though it may have been on this occasion that she made her peace by presenting the Queen with an incomparably expensive dress, elaborately embroidered with flowers and animal and insect creatures, such as became fashionable later and may be seen in portraits of the 1590s. Bess's wealth enabled her to keep Elizabeth sweet by exceptionally welcome New Year gifts, kirtles of yellow satin embroidered all over with 'purled silver', tawny satin laid with Venice lace and gold buttons. She did not lose the Queen's favour: 'there is no lady in this land that I better love and like'. Or it was, 'that good couple show in all things what love they bear me'. Shrewsbury, growing older, became her 'faithful old man'.

On Charles Lennox's early death in 1576 it fell to Bess to follow up his rights to the earldom, and the lands, of Lennox and the jewels that went with it. Eventually King James was able to bestow these upon his beloved cousin, Esmé Stuart, the Daubigny who was to initiate him into the more sophisticated delights of the Court of Henri III, a change from the Presbyterian rigours (and the cane) of his tutor Buchanan. Shortly the young widow, Bess's favourite daughter, died. Shrewsbury reported, 'my wife, although she acknowledges no less, is not so well able to rule her passions, and has driven herself into such a case by her continual weeping as . . . she being now at Chatsworth, I am desirous to go to her for a while'. The Earl had to take the Queen of Scots and her train along with him. Undiscouraged, Bess now transferred her campaign for the Lennox inheritance to her 'jewel', the little Arbella. They never got it out of James.

We see that Bess was a woman of warm affections, if concentrated within the family, a large and growing one. Grief did not prevent that forward-planning head from conceiving a very important alliance for her royal grandchild, aged eight in 1583. Leicester was no less ambitious than Bess and had at length achieved a legitimate son and heir, though the Queen had held up a satisfactory marriage and family life for him for years. By his secret marriage to her cousin, Lettice Knollys (of whom she was understandably jealous, having no fun herself), Leicester now had his little boy, Robert, to offer. Mary Stuart was the first person to pass on the news, which might have caused trouble if it had taken effect. But Leicester's hopes died with the 'noble imp', as he is described on his tomb in the Beauchamp chapel at Warwick. A little lame, he had been a page of honour to the Queen: one used to see his diminutive suit of chain-mail, alas, in Warwick Castle before its historic treasures were dispersed in the general ruin of our time.

By this time a breach was widening between Shrewsbury and Bess. The various strains upon him were too much for him to carry. He was not of a happy nature, querulous and irascible, and not particularly intelligent; one can see from his letters that he had a sense of inferiority in regard to Bess's formidable personality. His was weaker: he had the obstinacy of a weak man, where she had the persistence of a strong-minded woman. On the other hand he was a noble earl, of an ancient family; she was ennobled only by marriage to him. He was a dynast in being, head of all the Talbots; who were the Cavendishes? He did not appreciate that Bess was a dynast too, but planning for the latter.

Henry's future as the heir was provided for with Chatsworth, at the time occupied also by Bess and the Earl. But Henry had no children by Grace, the Earl's daughter – promiscuous and spendthrift, he had a number of bastards instead. He was not approved of by Bess. The only good thing known of him is a remarkable journey he made overland – through Dalmatia and the Balkans – to Constantinople. Very few, if any, Englishmen did such a thing at the time; the evidences of it that remain are a journal kept by his attendant and a few Turkey carpets still at

Hardwick. Bess's hopes were pinned on William, a son after her heart, an able business head on whom she could rely, who gradually became her aide and deputy in their multifarious affairs. For herself and him she bought her old home, Hardwick, from her failure of a brother who had not been able to manage it and died bankrupt in the Fleet prison. She paid £9500 for it outright. There remained Charles to provide for: a third house and estate would be needed for him in the future.

Charles was a different character again, gay and outgoing extrovert and friendly – he was a life-long friend of the Earl's second son Gilbert, with whom he travelled abroad. Gilbert was extravagant, with not much of a head to him – any more than any of the Talbots had. In the quarrel that was brewing between the Earl and his wife, Gilbert and his Cavendish wife took Bess's side. The Earl's eldest son Francis died, leaving a load of debt and no children; Gilbert took his place in the succession, not in his father's affections, also handsomely loaded with debt.

Though Shrewsbury had princely possessions in land he was hard put to it for cash; with all these claims upon him, he too was buying land and building a place at Worksop. All very Elizabethan. His building became competitive with Bess's. We find him haggling with her for the service of their expert plasterer, Thomas Accres, employed upon the Chatsworth interiors. The Earl told Gilbert 'how often I have cursed the building at Chatsworth for want of her company by her going away'. On her part one notices a tendency to bicker even before the open breach between them, made by the Earl. She phrases her demand thus: 'if you cannot get my timber carried I must be without it, though I greatly want it'. She was sure that the tenants would not refuse her. 'I pray you let me know if I shall have the ton of iron: if you cannot spare it I must make shift to get it elsewhere.' She does not appear anxious for his company when she writes, 'come either before midsummer or not this year, for any provision you have yet you might have come as well at Easter as at this day. Here is yet no manner of provision more than a little drink, which makes me to think you mind not to come.' Then follows a postscript which may be joking: 'Let me hear how you and your charge and love doth, and commend me, I pray.'

The Earl was by no means a harsh keeper of the Queen of Scots; he put her up in his hall at Buxton and at this time she was at liberty to ride in her coach-and-six in Sheffield Park. But a joke on such a touchy subject, taken *au grand sérieux*, would have detonating consequences, and of course Mary Stuart took a hand in the growing breach. She imparted to the French ambassador in London, with her usual indiscretion, 'my intention of involving indirectly the Countess of Shrewsbury'. Equally, of course, everything of hers was opened.

The decisive cause of the breach was, however, financial. We cannot go into the details, even if they were all discoverable. The plain position was that, by the original settlements, large sums of money were accruing from the Earl to Bess and she was employing them to build up the Cavendishes – as the Earl wrote, 'they have sought for themselves and never for me'. This was only natural: Bess had law and right on her side. The only time when she put herself in the wrong was when she walked out on the Earl at Sheffield and made for Chatsworth. Shrewsbury took his opportunity – in modern terms it could have been construed as desertion – not to see her again, until forced to by the Queen's command. Bess said that her absence was better appreciated than her presence – and the Earl may already have found one of his women servants more easy-going company. He said that Bess scolded like 'one at the Bank', i.e. like a lower-class fish-wife, and that she mocked and mowed at him. No doubt she had a North Country sharpness of speech.

The breach came into the open when Shrewsbury sought to recoup himself by going back on the financial settlement of 1572, denying it and thus putting himself in the wrong. He tried to take over the Chatsworth estate and Bess's own St Loe estates in Gloucestershire and Somerset, instructing his agents to collect the rents. The tenants objected, and the disputes, public in themselves, required public settlement. There were affrays between the servants of the Earl and those of the Cavendishes; people took sides. In the family the Cavendishes held with Bess, but so also did the Earl's son and heir Gilbert and his wife. Shrewsbury made a demonstration against Chatsworth with his armed following; he was withstood and answered back by William Cavendish from the leads.

Both sides appealed to Queen and Council. On his side Shrewsbury put it that Bess, 'seeking to recompense my liberality with spite and disdain, she hath animated her son William Cavendish with weapons to deny me a night's lodging in Chatsworth . . . greatly to my dishonour. It were no reason that my wife and her servants should rule me and make me the wife and her the husband.' Here was the rub: the phrase reveals the Earl's sense of inferiority towards his wife. Shrewsbury was moody and emotional where Bess, who could be passionate, was yet firm and consistent. And it is obvious from the line that he took that he was not intelligent, for he took the law into his own hands. The case that he put in reams of letters to Queen and Council was simply emotional self-justification, subjective and unrealist.

Considering this, he was treated with much forbearance by Elizabeth and her leading councillors – Burghley, Leicester and Walsingham. They were all brought into it, for Earl and Countess were two great estates of the realm, upon whom rested the heavy responsibility of keeping the Queen of Scots safe and from doing damage. Elizabeth was much concerned on several counts: such an open conflict between man and wife at the top of society was insupportable – it set such a bad example. (Even in the late Victorian age Lord Salisbury when Prime Minister intervened in a similar breach, so that it should not come out into the open.) Three times the Queen intervened to settle the issue and get the Earl to take back his wife. Twice he ignored Elizabeth's expressed wish and obstinately refused to budge.

The danger of the rift was further pointed up when the scandal spread that Shrewsbury had been too familiar with his alluring prisoner and that Mary had borne him a child. No one knew whence the slander originated, nor does it matter, for it was just the kind of libel that ordinary people put about concerning the eminent in Tudor times (if not today). Again and again people said that Elizabeth had a couple of children by Leicester – she wisely took no notice of such rumours. But Mary Stuart, who

had had closer experience of such contingencies, or rather con-
crete acquaintance, was infuriated. Shrewsbury was wounded,
of course, in his 'honour'.

In 1585 he made a special journey to Court to plead his case.
Stupid as he was, he was undoubtedly convinced that he had
right on his side. It was a purely subjective conviction; the facts,
the law were against him; Queen, Burghley, Leicester all recognised that right was on Bess's side. She played her cards coolly,
and wisely kept silent, except for insisting on her desire to be
received back by the Earl and to live with him as his wife. The
Queen treated her 'faithful old man' with every consideration,
when he had twice taken no notice of her expressed wishes. Her
final award, however, could not but be in accord with justice
and was a shock to the Earl. Bess was to keep all the lands made
over to her by the settlement of 1572; William and Charles were
to retain the lands which had been properly purchased for them
under the settlement, i.e. with Shrewsbury's money; he was to
hand back £2000 from the rents he had illegally seized and to
drop all suits against the Cavendishes and their tenants. In
return Bess was to pay him £500. Altogether it was a bitter pill.

Finally, he was commanded by the Queen to take his wife
back – as she had made the Earl of Oxford take his. Shrewsbury
could not contest the award; he had formally to obey the
Queen's command and take his wife back to Wingfield.
Dejected, resentful and inwardly determined not to live with
her – love turned to obsessive hatred – he escorted her to
Wingfield, stayed there a day or so for form's sake, then
departed for good. Recriminations continued to flow from his
pen, though the Council had offered a sop to his wounded pride
by imprisoning William Cavendish for the affront to the Earl's
honour in keeping him out of the house at Chatsworth: 'it was
not meet that a man of his mean quality should use himself in a
contemptuous sort against one of his lordship's station and
quality'. Privilege must be observed, as when the chivalrous
Philip Sidney was made to give way to the worthless Earl of
Oxford.

Bess had much reason to be content with the award, though
she adhered to the strategic position of injured wife wishing to

live with her husband. This may well have been sincere, for Bess was in everything a family woman, as conventional in her views as the Queen herself, with whom there was a large area of common agreement and sympathy. However, it was usual enough to accept the fact that her husband – now freed from the overwhelming charge of the Queen of Scots – should retire to the manor of Handsworth on his Sheffield estate and console himself in the arms of Mrs Eleanor Britton. Just as Shrewsbury had had to preside at the condemnation to death of his friend Norfolk, so he had a gruesome duty to perform at the last tragic appearance of his charge, the Queen of Scots, upon the scene at Fotheringay. As Earl Marshal he had to give the signal for the axe to fall upon that scheming head which had brought him so much trouble: raising his baton of office, he turned away from the horrid spectacle.

With his obsession against Bess he withdrew from her vicinity. It has been usual to regard his last companion as a household servant, but Mrs Britton was a gentlewoman. Something of that may be glimpsed in the jewels she acquired from the old fool – far more than a mere servant would have annexed: gold chains, diamond rings, pearl buttons, gilt bowls, household goods and a mass of ready money. These depredations led to a series of law-suits, upon the Earl's death, with his heir, Gilbert; for the engaging Eleanor claimed that they had been gifts from her *inamorato*. The lady may have been a Catholic, for a witness deposed that Topcliffe – a kind of Protestant Inquisitor-General – offered the Shrewsburys to frame her as such. This they refused, for Bess's daughter, the new Countess, was a Catholic convert.

Inconsistencies never bother humans, and these family complications had not prevented the old Earl from pursuing prominent Derbyshire neighbours, like the Fitzherberts of Norbury, for their too conspicuous Catholicism, with several of the family active exiles abroad. And, in pursuing them, old Shrewsbury had not disdained the aid of the government's chief agent and authority on the subject, Topcliffe: no one knew more about recusant families and their ramifications, the Jesuits and seminary priests operating against the laws.

Recriminations continued between Bess and her husband into

his last years. He asked back the many gifts he had made to her in the early years of his infatuation: basins, ewers, salt-cellars, plates – even the embroidered copes we still see at Hardwick. For of course she did not give anything back. She returned a sharp reply: 'the parcels above demanded by the Earl are things of small value and mere trifles for so great and rich a nobleman to bestow on his wife in nineteen years'. It was true that the Earl was rich in lands, but she said nothing about the large sums that had accrued to her from him, which she had capitalised into lands for her Cavendish sons. He returned with an insulting reference: 'there is no creature more happy and fortunate than you have been; for, where you were defamed and to the world a byword when you were St Loe's widow, I covered those imperfections by my intermarriage with you and brought you to all the honour you have and most of that wealth you now enjoy'.

These aspersions cannot have been true, or the Queen would never have given Bess the certificate of good conduct and credit in her service all those years ago. In the last year of the Earl's life his bishop, the Bishop of Lichfield and Coventry, strove to bring man and wife together with a long letter of counsel in accordance with his calling. 'Some will say that the Countess is a sharp and bitter shrew. . . . Indeed, my good lord, I have heard some say so. But if shrewdness or sharpness may be a just cause of separation betwixt man and wife, I think few men in England would keep their wives long.' If this seems a little excessive, we must allow that clerics know the ways of human nature better than most. The good bishop had wrestled with Bess herself and obtained a promise that 'she will so bridle herself that way beyond the course of other women that she will rather bear with your lordship than look to be borne withal'. I detect a note of independence rather than of submission in that, an assertion of equality, where the Earl had expected her to confess that 'you have offended me and are heartily sorry for it, in writing, and upon your knees without either if or and'.

These are the accents of a weak man; for Bess we can reply in the words of Shaw's no less independent Eliza Doolittle: 'Not bloody likely.'

Shrewsbury was beyond rational persuasions, and shortly he

was beyond anything. He died on 18 November 1590, and was buried in great state in the splendid tomb he had prepared for himself in the family church at Sheffield, now the cathedral. In the inscription upon the monument Bess is not mentioned; but, in Latin for the benefit of posterity, he replies once more to the aspersions upon his keepership of Mary Queen of Scots. Touchy and vulnerable as ever, he should have taken no notice of them.

II

The Countess dowager of Shrewsbury was now free, richer than ever, and quite independent. She also had her fourth lot of widow's thirds, much the largest, to enjoy. By law and by right she was entitled to one-third of all the late Earl's disposable revenues for life – and no one could have foretold how exceptionally long that life would last: an important factor in building up the fortunes of the Cavendishes.

This at once led to a breach with the heir, Gilbert, hitherto friendly; for more than the next decade relations with him were acrimonious and disputatious. Gilbert found that his father left nothing like so much disposable cash as he expected, so much had been siphoned off to Bess and her family. In time the immense Talbot estates would be able to meet the bill, something like £3000 a year more for Bess. But meanwhile Gilbert, muddled and emotional like his father, tried to resist – he could not produce the cash, and embarked on law-suits with Bess (as well as with Mrs Britton). Bess as usual was legally in the right, but had – also as usual – to fight for her rights.

Gilbert was even more temperamental than his father; at one time he challenged his brother to a duel over the will, he engaged in other fights, and various local quarrels. Unlike his father he was thriftless. Why should Bess sacrifice her interests for his extravagance and improvidence? That would be in accordance with modern standards; it was not with Elizabethan.

In one crucial matter the late Earl had foretold rightly – that Bess's grandchild, Arbella, would bring grave trouble to his family. This was on account of his daughter-in-law Mary's devotion to her niece. The new Countess had her mother's scheming head, without her overriding sense of reality; moreover she was misled by her Catholicism. As Queen Elizabeth aged and the succession to the throne became a matter of crucial importance, Arbella, with her Stuart and Tudor claim, became the candidate favoured by a considerable section of Catholics.

Arbella had been well educated, particularly in languages, Latin, French and Italian, and she read a good deal. At her first visit to Court it was disappointing that 'her Majesty spoke to her, but not long and examined her nothing touching her book'. However, the Queen raised hopes by pointing her out to the French ambassador, saying that the girl would one day be 'even as I am'. This helped to turn Arbella's head; she was too young to appreciate the political inwardness of this – a hint to keep James of Scotland in line.

On her second visit to Court Arbella displeased everybody by her insistence on taking precedence over everyone as a royal princess, unrecognised of course by the Queen. How like her great-aunt Mary Stuart this was! And indeed Arbella was a complete Stuart: she had the charm and the fantasy, with her head in the air, her feet were not quite on the ground. On this occasion she was ordered from Court with a flea in her ear, back to her grandmother who now had all the trouble and care of her.

Arbella had another of Mary Stuart's characteristics: along with her fantasying she had extreme persistence, a psychotic obstinacy in her fantasies, and she would never take telling. As we have seen, the marriage of persons of royal blood was a matter of state. Arbella became fixed on a marriage with Edward Seymour, whose whole life was overclouded by his father's marriage to Lady Jane Grey's sister, of Tudor blood, Henry VIII's niece. A Stuart–Seymour marriage would fortify Arbella's claim.

Arbella's scheming had the consequence – again as with Mary Stuart – of only getting her more closely watched than ever, and Bess had another such assignment in her old age. When one

goes to Hardwick one sees the little chamber within her grandmother's where the girl slept. She tried again and again to
escape, with the connivance of Bess's 'bad son', Henry, and a
Catholic agent, one Stapleton. Bess became sick of her charge
and the trouble she gave – the situation ruined relations between
them; the old lady must have been relieved when Arbella was
rusticated to the Earl of Kent's charge.

No doubt it was through the Kent family that Emilia Lanier –
Shakespeare's Emilia – was acquainted with Arbella; for as an
orphan Emilia had been brought up by Susan Countess of Kent.
When Emilia Lanier published her long religious poem, a
couple of years after the unwelcome publication of the much
earlier Sonnets, a dedicatory poem to Arbella was included:

> Great learned Lady, whom I long have known,
> And yet not known so much as I desired:
> Rare Phoenix, whose feathers are your own,
> With which you fly, and are so much admired:
> True honour which true Fame hath so attired. . . .[4]

Her position became a pathetic one: exalted, next after
James I's children, the candidate of conspiratorial Catholic
hopes, no marriage possible for her – even before the Queen's
death Bess would have welcomed a marriage to any commoner
to get Arbella off her hands and out of dizzy danger. Arbella
persisted and only a couple of years after Bess's death managed
to marry Seymour secretly. Their attempt to escape to the
Continent was aided and abetted by her aunt the Countess of
Shrewsbury, who fetched up in the Tower for her offence and
had to pay an enormous fine. Arbella herself died in the Tower.
The fine came out of the Shrewsbury estates – the old Earl had
at least been right in the trouble he foretold for his family.

But this is to anticipate. Bess had nearly eighteen years before
her in which to build up and up, expanding her operations in
complete control. The richest woman now in the kingdom, she
was really the head of a large business concern, based on land

but dealing also in cash. There were no banks in Elizabethan England and an acute scarcity of ready money, so she performed the functions of a banker, lending money on a large scale against the security of land, mortgages, land falling in to her; land purchases, purchases of tithes and advowsons, rectories and vicarages from the Crown; leasing out her lead and iron mines, working her own quarries. She sat at the head of the vast concern, like a Pierpont Morgan. One of her daughters married a Pierrepont: I do not know if there was any direct descent.

In all this Bess had her second son William as an active aide, becoming more and more her deputy. He had her business capacity and she trusted him implicitly, unlike her eldest son with his brood of bastards. Henry had no legitimate issue, so the prospect opened out of William succeeding to Chatsworth. Meanwhile she was adding on to her old home at Hardwick for William to succeed her there.

From the time of the final breach with the Earl she had been rebuilding the home of her fathers, bit by bit as money came in. It had a fine situation on the edge of an escarpment with a grand westerly view over Derbyshire. She raised the centre of the old house, and then equipped it with two large wings. The result was that the tall house had an irregular frontage, but as she proceeded she gave it fine interiors.

Building was the real passion of her life – that and her family: the two were intertwined, the buildings were to house her dynasty. It was an ambition completely characteristic of that ambitious age, which has left its lasting memorials of it, as against the trivial consumption of the demotic society of today. Her friend, the great Lord Burghley, accomplished and expressed his inner ambition in the building of Burghley for his elder son's line, and for the younger's Theobalds, which Robert Cecil exchanged for Hatfield.

It was the eighteenth century that left Old Hardwick to ruin; but as one looks up into the interior one can still envisage the grand lofty rooms Bess gave it, with the peeling friezes and giant figures of her plasterers and carvers. These may be seen as training for the new Hardwick she was able to put in hand with the Earl's death. It stands but an arrow-shot from her old home, worked on by the same masons, craftsmen, artists – and yet a contrast in so many ways. For one thing it has symmetry, a certain perfection; she seems to have got a 'plat', a master-plan, from the most remarkable of Elizabethan architects, Robert Smythson, who had already worked at soaring, but less perfect, Wollaton.

Nothing gauche about the new Hardwick: compact and integrated, not huge and spread out over courts like Burghley or Theobalds or later Audley End, it yet expresses even more the fantasy of the age. This is largely due to the tall turrets, six of them on the roof-line, linked by the balustrade with its signature: ES. ES. ES. with her arms and coronet. The place too has entered into folklore, like its creator: 'Hardwick Hall, more glass than wall.' One should see it with the sun going down, all the west windows aflame in the sunset. An Elizabethan interior would be brilliant with prime colours, everything rich and painted; black and white marbles, red and gold, blue and green – now all faded to the moonlit hues we prefer. And indeed one should walk the galleries and corridors as I have done, up the stone staircase by moonlight, the half light filtered eerily along the steps, passing the shadowy corners, past the small chapel off the main stairway, into the long gallery with its portraits of Bess and those who knew her in her day, the rival Queens, Burghley, Leicester and the Stuarts. The place that once was so full of life is empty and echoing now, yet alive with the shivering sense of their ghostly presences watching – to anyone who knows them and has historical imagination.

In summer I have sat there beneath her portrait – the long face, ruffed and coiffed with hanging gold chain – day by day turning over the pages of her accounts, signed weekly by the old lady with her large affirmative signature: *E. Shrowesbury*. Among the mass of papers, inventories, wills, letters, notes hoarded up by the methodical Bess one comes across an occasional scrap that brings those vanished lives back to one with a jolt. Amid account books innumerable these are real people. Here is the soldierly Sir William St Loe's will, bequeathing to his 'most entirely beloved wife, Dame Elizabeth St Loe . . . all manner his leases, farms, plate, jewels, hangings, implements of household, debts, goods and chattels whatsoever'. Here are his letters to Bess, a copy of his replication to his brother on leaving her everything.

More moving is the will of Bess's favourite daughter, Elizabeth Countess of Lennox, dying young and bequeathing to her mother's care Arbella, 'the solace of my life'. As late as 1604 a note tells us that 'my lady is this night informed by a gentle-woman here that a gentleman of credit now here saith there is no good agreement between Mr Henry Cavendish and the lady his wife; and that he hath lately charged her to be a harlot to some of his men and named the men to her'. A charming note is struck, on the more satisfactory side of the family which con-solidated the name: in 1602 William promises his boy of eleven a rapier and dagger, an embroidered girdle and spurs, if he will speak Latin with his cousin Arbella until Lent Assizes. The promise is signed by both father and boy.

The portraits in the Gallery bring alive once more the people who surrounded Bess and made that long career what it was. Here is the Earl, to whom after all she owed her grandeur: long aristocratic face, light brown hair greying, neatly parted in the middle, wearing the Order of the Garter; aged fifty-eight in 1580, painted just when things began to go badly wrong. Sir William Cavendish is much in contrast: heavily jowlled potent type, podgy, with shrewd unfriendly Henrician eyes; thick nose in fleshy face, long beard coming to a point; black cap and furred gown, painted when forty-four. Next, Sir William St Loe: bald, easy-going old person, fair hair and blue eyes: easy game for a woman like Bess – here she is, long slender hands, hand-some hawk-like face, ready to pounce. Then the unsatisfactory heir, Henry Cavendish: a foppish young man with French cap and pink plume, long nose and pointed beard; high collar and little ruff; a piquant birdlike expression watching; hair light brown with a touch of his mother's red. Next, his wife at nineteen, Grace Talbot, a dumpy little figure in black, the virgi-nals beside her and an open book of music. I think she was a little deformed: at any rate no children.

The portraits of the royal Stuarts Bess became so closely

connected with demonstrate her ascent unparalleled in that age: the tall picture of Mary Stuart in mourning, in the tenth year of her captivity. Another of her with Darnley, whom Bess may have met at Elizabeth's Court; and of course the Queen herself whom she knew so well and with whom she saw so much eye to eye – self-disciplined, controlled, eye on the main chance. Here too is another tell-tale relic: a green silk cushion worked with beautiful designs by Mary to while away those hours, with Bess performing a useful function in occupying her mind and keeping an eye on her.

Among the inventories is one of 'household stuff which is appointed by this my last will and testament to be, remain and continue at my house at Chatsworth'. In Mr Henry Cavendish's bed-chamber we note a cushion of Turkey work and a quilt of carnation taffeta; his chamber was wainscotted with a further chamber within. Next was Gilbert Talbot's chamber with a bedstead painted green. 'In the withdrawing chamber to the Scots' Queen's chamber – a board covered with green cloth, a coverlet and a closet there wainscotted.'

Bess designated also the furniture to remain at 'my house or houses at Hardwick'. In her time both houses were kept going, complementary to each other, with a household of some sixty people to maintain both. Two of the turrets on the leads of the new house were used as store-rooms, one for bedsteads and their furniture, another for pewter and cutlery. The Pearl Bedchamber (now the Blue Room) had and still has the Planets tapestries; in the Wardrobe chamber a quilt of yellow India stuff embroidered with birds and beasts, white silk fringes and tassels; in the green bedchamber a colour scheme of green and yellow, window curtains to match; in the stair chamber gilt leather hangings twelve feet deep. The best bedchamber had a large sparver (i.e. canopy) and bedshead with valences of cloth of gold and silver, sundry colours of velvet embroidered with arms and figures; deep gold fringe made from the copes from Lilleshall (now in the hall). Three-foot Turkey carpets lay about the bed.

We cannot go into the inventories of all those chambers, the rare pieces of inlaid furniture, the numerous tapestries and hang-

ings of cloth of gold, cloth of tissue, the embroidered figures of
the virtues: Zenobia for magnanimity and prudence, Artemisia
for constancy and piety, Cleopatra for fortitude and justice,
Lucretia for charity and (somewhat paradoxically) for liberality.
Tapestries of Penelope and Ulysses, and the whole story of
Gideon; needlework panels of Astrology, Logic, History, and
Perspective Arithmetic; panelling with insets of Roman
emperors; Renaissance tables of marquetry, inlaid with instruments of music – several of the Cavendishes were devotees of
music. It is all the Elizabethan version of High Renaissance, the
classical still intermingled with Gothic, provincial but vigorous,
abounding with life and self-confidence, above all the sense of
achievement.[5]

In the 1590s the dowager Countess was, in modern terms, a
millionairess. We can give only a small sample of her financial
transactions. The Earl of Cumberland, who spent so much
money on voyages and privateering – usually unremunerative –
mortgaged his lands at Edensor to her; thus they came to the
Chatsworth estate. For £2050 she bought all Edward Savage's
lands in Stainsby and Heath; for some £3000 Thomas Shaker-
ley's Little Longstone and all his lands in the Peak. Neighbour
Hercules Foljambe sold all his lands at Chesterfield, Moorhall
and Whittington to Bess for £1500; son William delivered him
the moneys in instalments. Godfrey Foljambe also appears as a
borrower – he must have spent a lot on his splendid tomb,
where we see him, in Chesterfield church. Among neighbouring families who resort to Bess for cash, like a banker, we note
Shakerleys, Sacheverells, Willoughbys, Markhams, Leeks, Fer-
rers, Fitzherberts – naturally upon the security of land. (Her
bedchamber was encumbered with coffers of cash.)

In spite of their quarrel Bess advances £1000 to Gilbert, the
new Earl, in 1593, upon bond with Sir George Savile; then
£1000 to Sir George Savile upon bond with Mr Portington.
And when Gilbert and his wife take the trouble to visit the old
lady he gets an outright gift of £100 and 'their three daughters,
every one £5'. To Edward Talbot, with whom querulous Gilbert quarrelled, she lends £200 on Midsummer day 1595; to Mr
John Stanhope, in spite of unfriendly relations, £200 upon bond

with Mr Wright. Bess delivers to son William £200 which Sir John Byron borrows,[6] and another £200 for Mr Foljambe of Walton. 'John Home, besides his rent of Eaton and Pilsley is to pay my Lady before Easter £220 which my Lady lent him.' There are unnumbered smaller loans we cannot go into – such a tell-tale item as an entry, in Bess's own hand, of 5s, 'given to Ralph White when I made the bargain with him for his lands'.

Nor can we go in any detail into her financial dealings with her family; we must, however, emphasise that Bess was generous, and not only to her family. The fact was that she was made on a big scale, and just as she was acquisitive on the grand scale so too she could be expansively generous. She provided each of her younger sons with a basic £400 a year, apart from the lands she purchased to endow them; in addition she made them regular gifts and upon occasion exceptional ones. She maintained, brought up and educated her royal granddaughter, and fought her battles. Bess tried hard to get for her her mother's £400 a year from the Crown, in lieu of the Lennox estates which James VI detained; Queen Elizabeth knew that Bess was well able to maintain Arbella and so would never award her her mother's pension in addition to her original allowance of £200 a year. We find Bess giving her granddaughter £500 to invest in land in Lincolnshire, or lending her a couple of hundred. On one occasion Arbella is given £100, a large sum in those days, to enlarge her pearl chain; in her will Bess left her all her pearls and sables, with £1000 down. She had taken over a number of properties Sir Francis Willoughby of Wollaton mortgaged to her for £3000, in Arbella's name: when they came to her they would be worth far more. A fine investment – unlike the Earl's purchase of Bess's original Barlow dower lands, which did not repay the purchase price. That showed the difference between her business ability and his lack of it.

In the accounts we find gifts great and small, fairly frequently £20 to Henry Cavendish; or, 'to Henry for a lease sold to Charles, £200'; 'to Charles, two obligations of Harry's, £310', for now the youngest son must be built up, and when he begins his building at Kirkby Bess starts him off with £100. 'To my son [i.e. in law] Pierrepont £50 to take up £500 towards a purchase he mindeth.' 'Given to little Will and Charles Cavendish 4 angels each: £4; to their nurse 10s.' 'Given to my daughter [i.e. granddaughter] Stapleton, £10: £5 for herself, and £5 to Gilbert to buy books withal.' 'Given to my cousin Chaworth, £5': this seems to be the regular gift upon a visit from a less close kinsman. One gets the impression that the old lady was a perfect milch-cow for them all: they all knew there was plenty of money there. She was not to be taken advantage of, however, or trifled with: fond as she was of her half-sister, Jane Kniveton, she notes, 'Given to George Kniveton, not in respect of his service but for his mother's sake over and above his wages, at my putting him away: £40.' This was a handsome handshake for an unsatisfactory attendant; it seems to have been regular form, for we find the entry, after payment of wages to a servant due at Christmas, 'given to Gurney at her going away, not for good service but for charity, 40s'.

On 2 August 1593 the old gossip Roger Manners was writing to Robert Cecil, 'yesterday was appointed the day for a marriage betwixt my nephew, George Manners, my lord your father's servant, and Mistress Grace Pierrepont at Chatsworth, effected by the old Countess. Wherein, I assure you, I was no party'. It sounds an unfriendly note; but in fact it was very good of the old lady to find a husband for one of four Pierrepont granddaughters. Sure enough, when we look into the accounts we see that Bess provided a handsome dowry: 'given to Mr John Manners with the marriage of Mistress Grace Pierrepont unto his son George, £700. To George Manners to buy plate against setting up house, £100.' And when the young couple come to visit the grandmother one day in May, they are given £20.

Nor is she less kind to her servants; when an upper servant, who has her confidence, marries Bess makes a contribution to setting her up – Mrs Digby the housekeeper, for example, was given as much as £60; or 'given to Lil at her marriage £40 in gold'. Every week a sum of money is distributed at the gate of Hardwick or Chatsworth or wherever she is in residence. 'To twenty poor men and women about Chatsworth to buy them coals, £6. 13s. 4d., to twenty poor children for the same, £4.'

When the old Countess moves about the countryside she moves in state, like the great personage she was. 'To my Lady at her going from Hardwick to Wingfield to be given to the poor, £20, of which William Cavendish to give the poor of Derby, £5.' 'At my Lady's going to Woodthorpe to gather her rents', for example – Dean that gathered them received 5*s*. for his pains: 'To the poor in Bolsover, 10*s*.; ringers there, 5*s*.' – for her approach was heralded by ringing the church bells – and cash was distributed everywhere she went, considerately but not improvidently. More money was distributed to more deserving persons: 10*s*. to the scholars, 11*s*. to the housekeeper at Woodthorpe, and more to individuals, maidservants, a nurse, a shepherd, and so on.

She made her contributions to what were regarded as good works. She paid for the bread and wine for Easter communions at Ault Hucknall, and 'given to Mr Chapman, the parson of Hucknall, for me and those that received with me, 10*s*.'; or, when in London, 'given for my lady Arbella and Mr Cavendish unto the parson of Chelsea for their communions, 10*s*.' To the bishop of Bristol's three sons, 40*s*. in all. 'To St Thomas' Hospital, at the feast of St Martin in winter last, £17. 15*s*. 7*d*.' – she must have paid for it. 'To Mr Broadbent towards maintaining his brother at the university, £20.' She sometimes shells out for sermons: 'To Mr Bennet, minister of All Hallows, Derby, for making a sermon this Good Friday, and his careful looking to the same almsfolk' – she was setting up her almshouse for twelve poor folk there – 'to see they keep good orders, 20*s*.' She donates money to the free school at Ashbourne, £10; or 'given to Hatfield of Alton toward maintaining his son at school, £5'; then a large sum to 'the bishop of London towards purchasing certain lands at Paul's Cross towards maintaining certain learned men of the universities to preach at Paul's Cross, £100'.

Regular payments were made, of course, for taxes, though these were in small proportion to either her wealth or her charities and good deeds; these last were made possible because the first was not eroded by penal taxation for the benefit of slackers and constant strikers as today. In our society, for all its waste on social services, the Christian virtue of charity has all but died out.

Much larger sums were sent to London by way of gifts, usually by William Cavendish. A regular ritual of the Elizabethan year was the giving and receiving of New Year gifts, from the Queen downwards. This was quite a business in itself. In earlier years Bess made particular gifts, a grand jewel or an expensive gown, and received back usually plate; later she gave varying sums, sometimes £100, sometimes £60. Here we have a sample from the 1590s: for the Queen twenty new pieces of gold, £40, for Lord Treasurer Burghley £20, Mr Secretary (Robert Cecil) £20, Lady Stafford £10, Lady Cheke a gilt bowl, £6. 15s. 10d., Lady Skidmore a gilt bowl and cover, £5. 3s.; Mr Attorney £10 and Mr Maynard £5. 17s. 6d. These were lawyers and sometimes the Master of the Rolls appears – it was necessary to keep them sweet. Legal expenses were a constant and large item, for in the undeveloped state of the law titles to property were often complicated and confused.

Back came the Queen's New Year gift, evidently a jewel or piece of plate, for the Master of the Jewel House received a reward of 30s., and Robert Saywood 8d. for carrying it to Mansfield. Red-deer pies, large affairs, also went up to London in considerable number: ten such to Mr Fanshawe and Mr Osborne, who were officials of the Exchequer, weighed eleven stone, carriage paid 12s. 10d.; four more went up to Mr Attorney and three to Lady Cheke. In February of this same year 1599 Bess paid £100 to the 'Receiver of the subsidies of the nobility . . . being the third entire subsidy granted to her Majesty in anno 39' (i.e. 1598).

At home New Year gifts were no less the order of the day: Henry, William, Charles and Arbella each received £20, Bess's daughter Frances Pierrepont, £40; sister Kniveton £13. 6s. 8d., George and Mary Kniveton £3. 6s. 8d. each; Mrs Digby £3, Lil 20s. and other servants proportionably. Altogether Bess paid out at home £147. This, however, was small beer compared with the purchases the millionairess was able to make: 'Sent to London at two several times, with other moneys paid there by debtors, for divers lands and parsonages appropriate and advowsons, £12,855. 15s. 11d.' 'Remains in the hands of my son William Cavendish, 19 October 41 Eliz. [1600] £514. 8s. 2¾d., and lent him more £400.' 'Given my son William towards his building at Oldcotes £100, which was lent to Mr Fitzherbert and repaid to me.'

William, who was to become 1st Earl of Devonshire in James's reign, is a rather misrepresented man. As able a business head as his mother – though she was the creator – he was a person of much wider cultivation. Well read as she was in the book of life, she spent nothing on books. In her grand bed-chamber at the new Hardwick – the state bed all scarlet laid on with silver lace, gold studs and thistles, tapestry hangings with personages and forest work over fifteen feet deep – were her few books: 'Calvin upon Job covered with russet velvet, the Resolution [this was the Protestant version made of Father Parsons' book], Solomon's Proverbs, a book of Meditations, and two other books covered with black velvet.'

William's interests were wider: we find him buying Gilbert's classic work on the Magnet, Stow's *Chronicles* and Carew's *Survey of Cornwall*; he buys too Guazzo's Dialogues, a book of Memorable Conceits, books and pamphlets in both Latin and Italian. Above all we notice his interest in music and the theatre. He buys all five parts of Luca Marenzio's madrigals and Morley's Songs of four parts. He performed himself, for there are regular purchases of singing books and lute strings, along with a treble viol. When in London he frequently went to plays, as well as to a sermon, sometimes paying extra for 'a stool to sit down on', evidently on the stage. How much we should like to know the plays he saw! Payments for tobacco appear, for, regrettably, he smoked. We must remember in his favour, however, that he was responsible for employing the philosopher Hobbes as tutor for his son and giving him a lifelong home with the Cavendishes. At Hardwick Hobbes occupied one of the tall lightsome turret rooms, where he could sing to himself to his heart's content to exercise his lungs – and was eventually buried in the tomb with its simple stoic inscription in the church by the park-gate at Ault Hucknall.

Charles Cavendish was a more popular character, living at some remove from his mother, since he was Gilbert Shrewsbury's closest friend. Sufficiently equipped with lands by Bess, he was able to marry the Ogle heiress. He eventually acquired Bolsover, building the extraordinarily imaginative great gallery and riding-school there along the escarpment looking across to Hardwick – now an eloquent ruin from the odious Civil War. He rented Welbeck from Gilbert, and later bought that too. He became ancestor of the dukes of Newcastle as well as of Portland, as William was of Devonshire: the three Cavendish dukedoms they all owed ultimately to Bess.

We derive from the accounts an even more vivid impression of life in the household occupying the two houses, the comings and goings of family, friends, neighbours; the noise and frolics, horses, stables, smells. When Charles is hurt – presumably in the feud with the Stanhopes – the eminent surgeon Clowes is sent down by the Queen's appointment to attend to his wound.[7] The old lady becomes arthritic and eventually hobbles about on a stick, head as clear as ever. 'Given to Doctor Hunton at his being with me when I took my physic, £3; to Digby at the taking of my physic, 40s.' But this is an almost unique entry: with her extraordinary vitality Bess continued healthy and active. A good deal of music entered into the life of any Elizabethan great house. Henry Cavendish had his own musicians at Chatsworth and occasionally sent them over; or Bess paid a quartet of men and boys for singing – evidently four-part songs. 'Given to them that plays of music with Will, 20s.' We have visits from Lord Morley's musicians, four of Mr Pierrepont's, the Earl of Rutland's or the Earl of Essex's; or from local minstrels, the waits of Nottingham and Doncaster, or the musicians of Lincoln. Occasionally a small troupe of players appears, Lord Thomas Howard's or the Earl of Pembroke's: they receive a mere 3s. 4d.

The weekly household accounts were viewed and signed by that firm hand, growing larger with age and failing eyes: *E. Shrowesbury*. The wages bill amounted to an average of £150 at each half-year, Midsummer and Christmas. The building accounts have been more studied, and we need not go into them here – so much material came out of her own properties, her quarries for the stone, her own lime for plasterwork, Derby-shire marble for chimney-pieces, her own craftsmen and plasterers who had been working for her for years upon Chatsworth, old and new Hardwick, and now Oldcotes which William was building for himself four miles away. Her domestic chaplain, Sir Harry Jenkinson, was clerk of works at Hardwick, evidently reliable and much trusted over years. Work upon the new house went on rapidly now that Bess was free; before it was finished – indeed it never was completely finished in every detail – she decided on a last visit to London to buy the equipment for it, a vast expenditure. It took place in 1591–2, the year after the Earl's death, and occupied almost a year: it was in a way a celebration of her freedom.

She travelled in her litter like an Oriental potentate. A couple of oxen and forty sheep were driven up to feed the household that collected at Shrewsbury House in Chelsea. This old-fashioned Tudor house with its courts occupied the area of Cheyne Row and Walk – very convenient for the main high-way, the Thames, up and down to Court at Whitehall and Greenwich. We can trace Bess's progress from her personal accounts 'at my Lady's setting forth from Chatsworth, Friday 20 August', ferrying her over the Trent at Sawley ferry, on to Loughborough that night, Leicester, Northampton (where pears were bought for 1*d*.); along Watling Street to Newport Pagnell, St Albans and Barnet, to arrive at London on Tuesday 24 August.

We catch something of the style, the show and clatter of the age in the payments to trumpeters, not only the Queen's but the Lord Admiral's. Frequent payments are made for boat-hire up and down the river, on one occasion the Bishop of London, a neighbour at Fulham, lends his barge; for the carriage of Bess's litter over the Thames, the hire of two litter horses, boats to Greenwich and back. For her New Year gift to the Queen a very splendid gown was being made by Johns, her Majesty's tailor, for which he was paid £59. 14*s*., while Par the embroi-derer was paid £50 for his work on it alone. Payments every-where Bess went tell their tale: to the Lord Admiral's cook and porter, the clock-keeper of the Queen's gallery, the keeper of the conduit at Greenwich, the Bishop of London's man that brought a Bible, to Shenton the fool and Ramsay the jester. It is like the *mise-en-scène* of *Twelfth Night* – and one sees, as always, how close Shakespeare's plays are to the life of the age.

A stay at Court at Greenwich entailed numerous payments there: to the Queen's gardener (one of them 'brought strawberries unto my Lady', and received 20*d*.), four of the Queen's Cellar and their servants, the waiters at the Buttery Bar and their servants, the Serjeant of the Queen's Pantry and one of his servants. Once and again the Countess is regaled with meat from her Majesty's Carver, or, brought by a page, meat from the Presence itself – a signal attention to the famous old lady. Visits were paid to her by her old acquaintance: the Lady Marquess of Northampton, Lady Warwick (the Queen's especial companion in these last years), Lady Southampton (mother of the young Earl), Lady Walsingham; among the men-folk the Lord Admiral, Lord Buckhurst, the Lord Chancellor, and Roger Manners. We can trace them from the payments made to their attendants. No wonder so many Elizabethan grandees were always in want of cash.

The old Countess was a collector rather than an aesthete. One of Mr Maynard's men brought a picture of the King of France, presumably that still at Hardwick. Enormous payments were made for glittering plates – one ruler of gold cost £100, silver candlesticks, gilt bowls, pots, standing cups, ewers, basins, looking-glasses, several gold chains, gold bracelets, silver boiling pots with covers, flagons, livery pots, posnets, spoons, casting bottles, bottles to hold cinnamon water. Considering all this the following seems little enough: 'given the 27 July 1592 to one Mr Hilliard for the drawing of one picture, 40*s*.' Obviously not enough, for there follows: 'Item, given unto the same Mr Hilliard, 20*s*.' Then, 'to one Roland [i.e. Lockey], for drawing another picture, 40*s*.' These would be miniatures, now worth thousands.

What did the old lady eat? Friday was a fast day, so on Friday 24 September we find: oysters 5*d*., lampreys 6*d*., shrimps 1*d*., half a saltfish 6*d*., a chicken 6*d*., a capon 2*s*. 8*d*., butter 9*d*.; grapes 4*d*., 3 pints wine 4½*d*., 1 quart French wine 4*d*. She had an apothecary in her service for the large household at £4 a year, but his gifts amounted to more, and he sold comfits, some of them of 'sweet fennel'. Rhubarb and liquorice were bought – better than the appalling concoctions of Elizabethan doctors: Bess did well to keep out of their hands.

While at Chelsea Mrs Digby gave birth, and was given 'at christening of the child, £4; the midwife and nurse, 10s. each; given by Lady Arbella, 40s.' The Countess attended to her legal affairs while at Chelsea, paid her bills of impost (customs duties, principally for wine), dealt with the Master of the Rolls and her attorney, while 'Mr Whalley laid out about my Lady's law matters, £40', a considerable sum. Far larger sums were laid out on cloths and stuffs, cloth of gold and silver, velvets, lace, canvas to back the hangings bought to glorify Hardwick – many of which are still there. Arras hangings displayed the Story of Abraham: 38¾ Flemish ells at 20s. the ell; another piece continued the story, 35 Flemish ells at 14s. an ell; a third piece measured 40 ells. The Story of Gideon required 17 pieces of arras, 1005½ ells at 6s. 6d., and cost £326. 15s. 9d., 'whereof for making new arms [her own] was bated £5 and likewise one half-stick [a measure], £321. 6s.' Bess took the opportunity to have a gorgeous new litter made, like the Queen's: yards of tawny velvet and tuft taffeta with deep gold fringe, tawny and gold parchment, gold and silk fringes – with a reward to him that sold the same.

For her return journey 'from Chelsea to Hardwick, 31 July to 5 August 1592', again we have the accounts: the usual payments to the poor, to musicians and to the bell-ringers that rung her in and out the towns and villages. The *cortège* was an impressive one, for she was bringing all the equipment she had bought for Hardwick, along with her personal store of cinnamon and spices, dates, rice, orris water, etc. It required 4 litter horses, 6 waggon horses, 39 hackney horses – by 'Norhampton' (evidently the old pronunciation) it had become 43 hackney horses, and by Leicester 45.

What is fascinating about her return journey is that she stopped to inspect various houses newly built, evidently with an eye to Hardwick, for comparison and improvement. She called at Sir William Hatton's Holdenby, the vast palace Sir

Christopher had built, which Lord Burghley admired with the eye of a connoisseur. It must have been then that she acquired the Hatton tapestries, 1200 ells of them, which remain a principal glory of Hardwick, with the Cavendish arms substituted for Hatton's. She stopped at the Pierrepont house at Holme in Nottinghamshire to see her daughter's family – £4 to 'the officers of the house'. Next at Wollaton, Sir Francis Willoughby's – who was away, for a mere 10s. was paid to the keeper and to one that opened Wollaton park gate, 4d.' Thus she arrived home in state, to carry on her multifarious family and business activities as usual, with the pleasure to look forward to of placing her treasures and equipping the new house that was her very own, her creation proclaimed to the world from the battlements – ES. ES. ES.

We have glimpses of her in these last years from the correspondence of the time, appealing to Robert Cecil – all powerful by 1600, against Gilbert Shrewsbury's attempt, 'under pretence of a grant of concealed lands,[8] to overthrow the estate of some lands formerly conveyed to her children, and dearly obtained by her, and upon great considerations'. In 1602 she was writing to Cecil in defence of her son – we do not know which – who had been summoned up on account of Thomas Gerard's 'complaint to the Queen of wrongs supposed to be offered him by my son'. Stout in defence of her family as ever, 'I doubt not it will fall out that my son hath and yet doth endure wrongs and hath offered none, and I trust he shall have redress. I am sorry to have been so troublesome of late but hope that mine shall, in justice, be righted as well in this matter of Mr Gerrard's as in the great wrongs the Earl of Shrewsbury hath offered them.'

Far more serious were the troubles caused by Arbella's schemes to get herself married and to escape from her grandmother's surveillance. The old affection between the two broke down under the strain. Arbella's temperament was precisely that of her great-aunt, Mary Stuart, who had taken notice of her as a child. Arbella was not without intellectual inclinations, she read much, but everybody observed her 'folly' – her beating like a bird at the wires of her gilded cage, her absolute refusal to accept the conditions of her existence, her inadequate grasp of reality, a certain light-headedness. When the scheme to marry Edward Seymour broke, the Queen sent down a commissioner, Sir Henry Broncker, to investigate – to whom Arbella lied and lied. It was just like Mary Stuart over again. Bess was deeply angered by the trouble and the danger of forfeiting good relations with the Queen; Sir Henry reported the old lady as 'wonderfully afflicted with the matter and much discomforted . . . she took it so ill as with much ado she refrained her hands'. Indeed, she must have been much relieved when Arbella was sent off into the Earl of Kent's keeping.

In September 1607 we have a letter to Cecil, now Earl of Salisbury, from Gilbert Shrewsbury – moaning as usual, like his father. 'My last pitifully complained of the gout's pinching me, and now you write of Tyrone and the rest their flying into Spain. But what is it to me, who am neither fit for counsel nor execution, but rather to live in a coalpit or a cell. . . . My wife has gone to see her mother; when she returns I will show her what you write of those that are so resolute against crosses, and wish she could in part follow their rare and excellent example.' These were the last months of Bess's life. In December Gilbert and Mary, with Charles Cavendish, went over to Hardwick, and 'there found a lady of great years, of great wealth, and of a great wit [i.e. intelligence] which yet still remains'. She received him 'with all respect and affection, and stayed them with her one day'. He returned 'without so much as one word of any former suits or unkindness, but only compliment, courtesy and kindness'.

With the forethought and due sense of order that had prevailed throughout her life, and made such a success of it, Bess was preparing for her demise. It was proper for a rich Elizabethan to leave a memorial that was also philanthropic – school, hospital or almshouse. Bess had built an almshouse for twelve poor folk, six men and six women, in Derby. We have all the accounts for building, slating and furnishing: twelve pairs of shovels and tongs, skillets, candlesticks, pewter dishes, brass pots; scores of yards of woollens for blankets, linen for sheets, bolstering, blue cloth for liveries; cans, cups, saucers, spoons; locks for the evidence chest, a characteristic touch. William goes to and from Derby about the business and Bess lays out £20 a year for her almsfolk, £12 for their liveries, £6. 13*s*. 4*d*. to Mr Bennett for a sermon on Michaelmas day.

Then her will and her tomb. She did not cut Arbella out of her will, for all the trouble she had given. Charles Cavendish's two sons were left 4000 marks to set them up in land. Queen Elizabeth was to have had a gold cup worth £200; James, now King in England, got it; the Lord Chancellor and the Archbishop of Canterbury £100 each in gold. Generous as ever to her servants, she left as much as £1000 for them, the favoured Mrs Digby receiving an individual bequest of £100. Bess did not wish for an 'over-sumptuous' funeral, 'performed with too much vain and idle charges'; but of course a personage of her rank and state would require due ceremony – a mere £2000 would suffice. She had the necessary moneys to perform her bequests counted out and placed in one of the coffers in her bedchamber. Her tomb was already prepared: she would not lie with the Talbots in their church at Sheffield, she would inaugurate her own dynasty in the parish church, All Saints, of her county town of Derby. There, in marble, she lies alone (where alone myself in the silence I have before now imprinted a chaste kiss on the cold forehead).

She died on 13 February 1608 in that bitter winter people long remembered. As she lay dying in her resplendent chamber, the flames leaping up in the grand fireplace, snow outside on the ground – folklore said that it was because it stopped her building that she died, such was the impression her personality made – she could reflect on the flickering, varying passages of her astonishing life, the loves and quarrels, the troubles and achievements; the menfolk in her life, pathetic young Roger Barlow with whom it all began, Sir William Cavendish who made her happy, kind St Loe who rendered her independent and rich, the Earl to whom she owed her grandeur, a person of state. The Derbyshire lass had moved and lived with Queens – Elizabeth Tudor and Mary Stuart, whose unsteady troubled course seemed to be echoing in that of Arbella. But at least the Cavendishes were safe.

SOURCES *Calendars of State Papers Domestic*; E. Lodge, *Illustrations of British History*, 3 vols, for Talbot correspondence; *Historical MSS Commission, Salisbury* and *Hastings MSS*; T. Wright, *Queen Elizabeth and her Times*, 2 vols; D. N. Durant, *Bess of Hardwick*, and *Arbella Stuart*; Hardwick MSS at Chatsworth.

2
Father Parsons the Jesuit

OTHING would have been more displeasing to Father Parsons than to be remembered as an 'Elizabethan', under the heading of the Queen of whom he was the most persistent and internationally famous enemy. Whatever he failed to achieve by his astonishing life's work of writing, teaching, political intrigue, he certainly was a European figure in his time, moving easily and dealing with kings and princes, cardinals and popes.

It would be ungenerous to deny him a certain genius; to have genius means to be obsessed by a spirit. Father Robert's obsession drove him relentlessly on – an outsize ego, great gifts for languages, diplomacy, politics; one of the best writers of Elizabethan prose, natural and easy, admired by Swift; an acute and dedicated controversialist; an immensely strong, unmistakable personality, complex and plausible, uncompromising yet tactful, capable of arousing ardent discipleship and a host of enemies. In short a fascinating psychological and historical study.

He was God's idea of a Jesuit: more than anybody else he created the idea of the 'jesuitical' that has haunted the English mind for centuries. A Catholic opponent, Father William Watson, wrote at the time of 'the most dangerous infections and irremediless poison of the Jesuitical doctrine'. One that made the worst impression was the casuistry of equivocation, which the *Oxford English Dictionary* defines as 'prevarication or mental reservation of the truth'. This achieved the headlines at the time of Gunpowder Plot – which was intended to blow King James and Parliament sky-high – about which the Jesuit Superior Garnet knew beforehand from confession, but said nothing.

William Shakespeare, who adhered to the ordinary Englishman's common sense about such matters, was writing *Macbeth* at the time, in which he described an equivocator as 'one that could swear in both scales against either scale, who committed treason enough for God's sake, yet could not equivocate to heaven'. And 'what is a traitor?' asks young Macduff; 'why, one that swears and lies', answers his mother. A few years later Purchas, the continuator of Hakluyt, wrote: 'easy it may be indeed to seared Jesuitical consciences that account treason religion'.

Here were the horns of the dilemma upon which the Jesuits impaled themselves in Elizabeth's England. Their aggressive campaign against the Elizabethan settlement of religion – the best consensus that could be achieved – in the circumstances of the war with Spain was directed against the polity and internal peace of the state, was contrary to the laws enacted by Parliament, which represented the country; and they themselves amounted to a fifth column in time of war. The state naturally reacted with every weapon at its disposal. The Jesuits *claimed* that they were acting solely for religion – though even the overthrow of the established religion would have meant the overthrow of the state. Actually, some of the leading spirits were up to their eyes in political action and conspiracy.

Once more William Shakespeare expressed the ordinary Englishman's point of view on this crucial issue: in Sonnet 124 he describes those who followed this course as

> the fools of time,
> Which die for goodness who have lived for crime.

That is – that though they regarded themselves as martyrs for religion, their actions, in these decades of war with Spain, were those of traitors. Of these, Father Parsons was the leader and instigator: for years he lent himself to the purposes of Spain. He was in the end a 'fool of time', for all his conspiring and intriguing came to naught: he died a defeated and somewhat discouraged man. But he had driven scores to their deaths, and was as much hated by the majority of his co-religionists, loyal enough, as he was by Elizabeth's government, which frustrated his knavish tricks and checkmated his incessant, obsessive activities. Their admirable intelligence system was very well informed about what he was up to.

No doubt he would have been equally willing to throw away his own brilliant life along with the others he led to the sacrifice. But does that make it any better?

I find him fascinating – infinitely more so than ordinary conventional people, even when they make some figure in history.

All kinds of things were said about Father Robert in his day, naturally enough about so 'controversial' a figure – in his case the cliché is apposite. We need not believe them – that he was illegitimate, for instance (what if he were?); that he was the son of a blacksmith (the more credit to him); that he was much attached to his own sex (what of that?). He certainly had a way with young men: he easily attracted those whom he liked to him – usually those of good birth and breeding, or good looks; others became as suspiciously jealous of him. He had a marked gift for friendship; he had good friends, but far more enemies, among Catholics quite as much as among Protestants, and across the Continent as well as in England.

He was born in 1546 – the last year of Henry VIII's reign – at Nether Stowey in Somerset, a village which remembers Coleridge's residence there, but has forgotten its native son. Parsons himself tells us in his *Brief Apology* that he was one of eleven children of very honest parents, his mother 'a grave matron living several years in flight and banishment for religion', and that his father had been 'reconciled by the martyr Father Bryant'. It would seem that he himself was the *fons et origo malorum* (or *bonorum*, according to taste): with his gift for leadership the family seems to have followed the lead of its brilliant son.

They had been Protestants, and the vicar of the parish helped to educate the promising boy, who went to school at Stogursey and then to the free school at Taunton. Thence to Oxford in 1564 to St Mary's Hall, of which his future collaborator, later Cardinal, Allen had recently been Principal, before leaving for Louvain and a lifetime of exile. Where Cambridge unfortunately developed a strong Puritan taint, Oxford was more conservative, with many Catholic sympathisers, and lost a number of distinguished men to exile.

Parsons became a Fellow of Balliol in 1568 and had much success as a tutor, with numerous pupils. This, as usual, aroused the jealousy of the inferior, particularly that of a junior Fellow whom Parsons had helped to elect, one Bagshaw. It is a familiar enough pattern to those who know the ways of college life. Bagshaw wanted to take over some of Parsons' pupils, in particular James Hanley, 'a very proper [i.e. good-looking] youth', and took him at 'a very tender age out to certain comedies at night', which Parsons had forbidden 'for fear of inconveniences that might ensue in such a throng'. Parsons was Dean; Bagshaw kept the boy shut up in his chamber for fear of the Dean punishing him.

Parsons called a meeting of the Fellows, at which he found himself outvoted by the great majority, of Protestant persuasion, led by the Master, who took the opportunity to charge him with perverting the youths of the house – religiously no doubt – and being backward in religion. Parsons was indeed dragging his feet, for though he had twice taken the Oath of Supremacy, he had not yet taken orders. Then there was a fuss about fasting in Lent, which he wished to enforce strictly; this went up to Leicester as Chancellor, who wrote back sharply, backing the Master. Parsons was persuaded to resign privately, rather than be dismissed publicly. He tells us that he was already treating to go overseas with a friend, John Lane, a Fellow of Corpus, who became a Jesuit in Spain. On Parsons' withdrawal – he was obviously too big a fish in a small pond – the Protestants rang the bells of St Mary Magdalen across the way (now *very* High

Church, more Catholic than the Romans) backward, as if there were a fire in the town.

It sounds all very trivial, but the consequences were by no means trivial. Parsons put the broils at Balliol down to Bagshaw, who eventually also became a Catholic and went overseas to Rome, 'where he showed himself the same trouble-maker and was dismissed'. This was true enough; he became a lecturer at the Sorbonne, returned to England as a seminary priest, spent years in prison at Wisbech, where he was a fomenter of further broils; after his liberation he lived and died in Paris. He was a person of no distinction.

Parsons spent some time in London, befriended by Thomas Sackville, then Lord Buckhurst. He had, with his intellectual gifts, a way of recommending himself to the great; but this brief association is of interest, for Sackville was the best of the early Elizabethan poets, author of the 'Induction' to *The Mirror for Magistrates* and part-author of *Gorboduc*, the first English blank-verse tragedy. Parsons intended to go to Padua and study medicine, on the proceeds of the sale of some land in Somerset given him by the parent of one of his pupils. He contradicted as a calumny of his enemies that he was a Catholic, and declared that 'he neither then was nor ever meant to be any papist'.

However, on his way through Louvain he was received into the Church of Rome by an English Jesuit. Arrived at Padua he did not remain long but set out on foot for Rome, where he offered himself to the Society of Jesus in the summer of 1575. He was no longer young; he was thirty, or in his thirtieth year – quite of an age to make up his mind finally. He had found his vocation thus belatedly, and after this never looked back.

Ordained priest in 1578, Parsons was given employment as English penitentiary in St Peter's and the care of novices at the English College in the Via Monserrato. From an ancient hospice for English pilgrims this had just been refounded as a college to prepare priests for the English mission, with the hope of re-converting England to Catholicism. This was the inspiration of the life's work of the stubborn Lancashireman, William Allen. Parsons' senior by some fourteen years, Allen had never compromised or accepted the Elizabethan settlement of religion, which proved to suit the country best. Allen took an aggressive line against the establishment everywhere, a strong influence in holding Lancashire for the old faith; abroad, he founded the college at Douai to receive students and give them a full Catholic education, many becoming missionary priests to upset the establishment at home.

Already in the English College at Rome conflict – which became endemic – was rife between the students and the infiltrating Jesuits with their itch for control. Parsons was instrumental in getting Allen to come to Rome to assuage the conflict, and thus began the historic partnership in the religious offensive against England which had such results, bloody as they were. The ecumenical spirit prevailing today can afford to admit how futile it was, with the loss of many good lives – for what?

The times were critical: the clash between the Spanish world–empire and the heretical half-an-island was approaching. Philip II, who had been king in England, was on the threshold of succeeding to Portugal, her overseas empire and ocean-going navy. Drake had penetrated into the Spanish preserve of the Pacific. The Desmond Rebellion in Ireland was set alight by James Fitzmaurice with support from Rome, under the spiritual direction of the exile Sanders: all Southern Ireland was aflame. Sanders was an improbably venomous Wykehamist and ex-Fellow of New College, a prolific propagandist against the English Reformation, writing a Latin work on the Progress of the English Schism, full of poisonous aspersions upon the Queen, and her mother and father. He was a catspaw of Rome and of Spain, a traitor.

In these circumstances there was understandable hesitation in Rome about adding Jesuits to the seminary priests being dispatched to England, as Allen and Parsons urged. In the end they won their plea, but the authorities laid strict injunctions that they were not to meddle with matters of state or discuss politics. Queen Elizabeth had already been rudely excommunicated and 'deposed' by the futile Papal Bull of 1570, which even Philip refused to have published in his dominions. The Jesuits were now given briefs to 'dispense' with the effects of the unfortunate Bull – this could of course again be revoked at leisure. What nonsense it all was!

The English government, with its excellent intelligence system, was shortly apprised of what was afoot. In the State Papers we find Burghley's characteristically careful and conscientious notes as to the effects of the faculties granted to Parsons and Campion for 'explication' of the Bull of Deposition. For these were the two Jesuits chosen to head the mission, Parsons as the busier working head to be superior though six years junior. Edmund Campion had had brilliant prospects at Oxford as scholar and orator. He had attracted the attention of the Queen by the grace of his delivery, and she recommended him to the protection of Leicester – at the demonstrative funeral of whose wife, Amy Robsart, Campion had preached at St Mary's. As a Fellow of St John's he had taken orders, but in some jealousy over preferment had gone to Dublin, where there was a project of founding a university. Here he wrote his Irish history, which is little but a tract to advocate education as the only means of taming the Irish. He was a precursor of Newman in his disappointment at the prospects there. In 1572 – the year of the Massacre of St Bartholomew – he made the pilgrimage to Rome to join the Jesuits, who sent him into Bohemia to serve his novitiate and there in Prague he was re-ordained.

Quite a little party of priests and chaplains left Rome with the two Jesuits, and the Pope's blessing – for what help that was – on 18 April 1579, and soon the English government knew the names of those to expect. The journey was made mostly on foot, and at Rheims Parsons met his brother George. The Flemish Jesuits were opposed to their invading England at this time, because of the unpleasant smell Sanders' activities had made for the Society, and the party thereupon decided to split up and land separately. Parsons landed first, a stout figure of a man, swarthy complexion, strong features which made a forbidding impression. This went well with his disguise of a returning soldier in captain's apparel, 'buff laid with gold, with hat and feather suited to the same', and attended by his man. Campion followed later, disguised as a merchant dealing in jewels, with a lay-brother for his servant.

Thus they passed the searchers at the port; though in the tilt-boat from Gravesend making for London at night, Parsons 'found himself in the midst of a company of gentlemen of the Inns of Court and some of the Queen's household with divers musicians, who had been to make merry in Kent'. In such company he might well fear discovery; but, safely arrived in London, he went to the Marshalsea, where a Catholic detainee put him in touch with George Gilbert, whom he had received into the Church in Rome. This rich young Suffolk gentleman was a fanatic who devoted the whole of his inheritance to the cause and a few years later died in Rome leaving the rest of his wealth as a legacy to the Church.

He was a help to Parsons throughout the mission, accompanying him most of the time and providing for him. Moreover, he was the centre of a knot of devotees who aided and supported the seminary priests and directed them along the network of families and sympathisers who wished to enjoy their services. When Campion arrived he preached an eloquent sermon in the crowded hall of Lord Paget's mansion, on the text 'Thou art Peter, and upon this stone [*petram*] will I build my Church' – a text exploited *ad nauseam* to anyone well read in these tiresome controversies. The audience it reduced to tears, for Campion was a moving preacher, where Parsons was the activist; the two of them appealed especially to the fervour of young men whose hearts they touched and whose confessions they heard.

Thus began the exciting story of the first Jesuit mission.

So open a flaunting of the government as the event at Lord Paget's was most unwise; when it was noised abroad that the Jesuits were in the country and at work, something like panic seized the authorities, who redoubled the search for them. This did not prevent a synod being held at Southwark, at which the new uncompromising spirit of the Counter-Reformation imposed itself upon the more moderate temper of the secular priests. The main issue was whether Catholics might occasionally attend the services of the Anglican Church. Southampton's grandfather, Lord Montagu, was advised by his priest, a learned man, that he might – and his house was a veritable 'little Rome' for the priests who sought refuge there. The Jesuits brought the strictest orders that in no circumstances were Catholics to attend church – it was 'peril to the soul' (whatever that may mean) and utterly damnable. The lines were rigidly drawn for battle. It was only to be expected that the government would reply in kind: it was its duty to defend itself against the new-comers.

After the synod the two Jesuits left on a missionary tour of two separate circuits, aided and abetted by their well-to-do young gentlemen. Parsons took the wider circuit of Northampton, Derby, Worcester and Gloucester, Campion that nearer London. The mission had marked success, Parsons for example 'reconciling' and absolving peers like Lord Compton and leading gentlemen like Dymock, the Queen's Champion. When one notes among those brought back to the fold such names as Catesby and Tresham, one sees the detonating long-term consequences in the Gunpowder Plot twenty years later. Meanwhile these people underwent fines, imprisonment and harassment for their fanaticism – unless they were peers, who were not interfered with, short of active treason.

We do not know the tally of all those who were reconciled, but it seems probable that the great composer William Byrd, of the Queen's Chapel, was one of them at this time – he had been like his senior, Tallis, an Anglican. Henceforth, though he wrote services for the Anglican Church, he did not support it – the Queen's tolerant favour saved him from prosecution. The success of the mission rather went to their heads: Parsons wrote that it was 'Father Campion's constant opinion that heresy in England was desperate, and few or no men of judgment did think in their consciences that doctrine to be true and defensible that was commonly taught and practised, the absurdities thereof being so many and manifest'. It was the typical mistake of an intellectual to think that doctrine and argument were of all that importance in a society. Parsons, like Lenin, understood that they were a weapon in the power-struggle, but that power was what mattered. Abroad, exiles with their *émigré* mentality took heart, buoying themselves up with false hopes: Allen at Rheims, whence he had had to decamp from Douai, wrote in

1581 that as a result of Parsons' and Campion's labours there were 20,000 more Catholics in England than the year before! Absurd as this was, the government was taking no chances.

To every aggressive step of the Papacy it replied in kind. The reply to the Bull of Deposition of 1570 was the Act of Parliament of 1571 making it treason to bring in Bulls and other dispensations, instruments and tokens of Papal power. The Jesuit mission of 1580 was now followed by Proclamations calling home English subjects from foreign seminaries, and by an Act of Parliament making it treason to reconcile the Queen's subjects to Rome, dispensing with her laws, and imposing a stiff fine of £20 a month for refusing to attend the Church of the land. It was in vain for Parsons and his like to appeal to liberty of conscience: where was liberty of conscience in Spain or under the Roman jurisdiction? Burned in the fires of the Inquisition, as English Protestants had been burned only a few years before under Philip and Mary.

On their return from making trouble for the government on their tours Parsons and Campion initiated their propaganda campaign through the press, acquiring a printing press and writing books and tracts which made a stir. Parsons now wrote the first of the numerous works that flowed from his prolific pen, mostly anonymous or under various pseudonyms, but easily recognisable. His first offering was a tract giving reasons why Catholics must refuse to go to Church, dedicated impertinently to the Queen – though it did condescendingly recognise her personal 'clemency in often staying the execution of the law', which was no more than the truth. He also began his full-time career as a controversialist by answering the confession of a priest who had sensibly recanted in the Tower, and refuting those Anglicans who had dealt with Campion's offer to dispute the issue.

Campion was anxious to appeal to their own university of Oxford, where most damage could always be done among naïf youthful minds. From a printing press concealed at Stonor near Henley, Campion's *Decem Rationes* was printed, with its statement of the Roman position, in time for Commencement at

Oxford. When the university assembled in St Mary's they were electrified to find the books distributed upon the benches.

People were alarmed at such effrontery; the government stepped up its efforts and made a round-up of suspects. Shortly Bryant was caught, a handsome young priest who had been Parsons' pupil; then Campion himself was betrayed. The government was unlucky, in a way, in catching Campion rather than Parsons; for Campion was a saintly man, not a politician. No one ever accused Parsons of being a saint, and he was always the politician.

The hunt was up and he made for the coast. He took refuge at Michelgrove in Sussex, the home of the Shelleys – all those Republicans, Shelley, Milton, Swinburne, came of recusant Catholic stock: anything to be out of step! With a party of Catholics, priests and laymen, Parsons escaped across Channel where he was safe. Every effort was made by the government to make Campion, now in the Tower, see sense. He and his companions supported and comforted each other in the Faith: all three were hanged at Tyburn in December, Campion, Sherwin and Bryant.

What a waste of human lives it was! It is said that a spatter of the martyred Campion's blood fell upon Henry Walpole, which – one must remember the credulity and superstition of the age – wrought his conversion. He, too, became in time a Jesuit martyr; almost the whole of that famous family was extinguished by its fanaticism. Which was a pity: if someone had not seen sense and conformed in time we should have been bereft of one of the ablest and most commonsensical of Prime Ministers in Sir Robert Walpole.

From his lair in Normandy Parsons proceeded to write a Latin tract on the persecution in England, and later a life of Campion. All this was useful propaganda for Catholic Europe as the cold war with Spain became open war, and it stoked up the fires of the cult of martyrdom which sent scores of good souls to their deaths. To be just, this may be regarded as the Catholic reply to John Foxe's book of Protestant martyrs, which was a best-seller in the Elizabethan age and helped to confirm Protestants in *their* faith. (What is an enlightened mind to think of either side in the regrettable conflict?)

From the security of the Continent Allen and Parsons built up the cult of the martyrs – much as the communists deliberately sent their faithful, willing or unwilling (my friend, Ralph Fox, among the latter), to become martyrs for their faith in the Spanish Civil War. The hangings and torture of Campion and many others, which shocked the civilised Victorians, have become so much more familiar in the decline of civilisation in our time. All this deplorable blood-shedding in Elizabethan England was rather superfluous – as John Donne, brought up in the cult of the martyrs, was later to demonstrate. Meanwhile, Donne's uncle, the Jesuit Jasper Heywood, who had been a Fellow of All Souls, was left by Parsons to take his place as Superior to carry on the good work in England.

Parsons spent the winter of 1581–2 at Rouen, a convenient post for English affairs and for forwarding priests on the mission. A new opportunity seemed to open up in Scotland with the arrival of young King James's French cousin, Esmé Stuart, who fascinated him and gained a hold upon him, which led to the fall and execution of the Protestant Regent, Morton. Parsons at once seized on this and dispatched Father Watts to work on the young King. 'On the conversion of Scotland depends every hope, humanly speaking, of the conversion of England.' Watts was well plied with arguments from Father Robert's fertile mind to urge upon James: 'the hope of succeeding to the kingdom of England, which he could obtain only through the aid of the Catholics' – the opposite was the truth; 'reverence for his mother who, though *void of offence*, had been driven out of the kingdom and confined to prison; the murder of his father by the heretics', and more to the same effect. In fact, Mary Queen of Scots' chief offence was not so much her involvement in the murder of her husband, but marrying the chief murderer, the heretic Bothwell, by Protestant rites. Father Robert was too plausible to be convincing.

In Normandy he was well placed for co-operation with the

Duke of Guise, leader of the aggressive wing of French Cath-
olics, whom he persuaded to endow a school for English school-
boys at Eu. This lasted until Guise's assassination by the Most
Christian King, Henri III, in 1588, when the school was transferred to St Omer: the direct predecessor of present-day
Stonyhurst. Guise was involved in the scheme for intervention
in Scotland known as the *Impresa* or Enterprise; Mendoza,
Philip's ambassador in England, was also behind the scheme.
Parsons drafted the Memorial to be placed before the Pope and
Philip II to gain their support. 'We ask for 8,000 infantrymen, or
at any rate 6,000 . . . together with money to pay a further 8,000
home troops for six months . . . to get the whole business
through. For there is no need for them to stay in Scotland, but,
as soon as ever the ministers are suppressed, they are to pass on
into England, before the Queen can overwhelm the Catholics
or prepare an army.'

So much for all the public protestations about not being
involved in matters of state: Father Robert had developed a
perfect itch for meddling in politics and marked gifts as dip-
lomatist and negotiator. He therefore was selected to journey in
the summer of 1582 to lay the plans before Philip, who was in
Lisbon absorbing his new kingdom of Portugal, with its fine
navy which would enable him to tackle the English at sea. By
this time affairs in Scotland had turned unpropitious with the
fall of Lennox (Esmé Stuart): once more the Protestants were in
control. The Pope and Philip, like the politicians they were,
dragged their feet, realising that there was no hope in this
Enterprise.

The Jesuit must have made a good impression on the Most
Catholic King, for henceforth he had Philip's good will and
personal support. He got out of Philip an annual subsidy of
2000 crowns for the seminary at Rheims, and an indication of
support for Allen's elevation to the cardinalate when the time
was ripe to settle accounts with England.

Father Robert was seriously ill in Spain. On his recovery his
energy was, as usual, prodigious. A brief visit to Rome secured
the renewal of Elizabeth's 'deposition' and Allen's appointment
as papal legate in England when the time came (it never did). At

home Francis Throckmorton was laid by the heels; his confessions blew the scheme of the Enterprise sky-high and revealed his traitorous dealings with Mendoza, who was ignominiously sent packing from the country.[1] Parsons moved on to Flanders where a regiment of English exiles was formed under the command of the Earl of Westmorland, who had survived the Rebellion of the Northern Earls in 1569. The Jesuit's advice was needed to provide chaplains and instruct the soldiers in Christian piety, charity, etc.

The summer of 1584 he spent mostly in Paris, with visits to Rouen to dispatch priests and equipment to Britain. In this work he co-operated regularly with Allen, 'he sending me priests from the seminary and I arranging, to the best of my power, for their safe transport to England'. Though his sights were trained on Oxford, he did not neglect Cambridge: 'at Cambridge I have at length insinuated a certain priest into the very university, under the guise of a scholar or a gentleman commoner and procured him help from a place not far from the town. Within a few months he has sent over to Rheims seven very fit youths.' No wonder Walsingham thought fit to infiltrate a Cambridge graduate into Rheims to see what they were up to – one Christopher Marlowe.

Since his return to France Parsons had transmitted material worth 4000 crowns to England, gifts to needy priests and no less than 810 books. A veritable industry of publishing English Catholic books on the Continent sprang up, instigated by the Louvain exiles, and by Allen and Parsons, who was an effective co-ordinator. He himself was writing all the time, conducting an immense correspondence with Allen, Aquaviva the Jesuit General, the English College at Rome, the Cardinals who were its protectors, besides that with his priests, agents and disciples. At this time he was writing his most important religious work, *The First Book of the Christian Exercise, appertaining to Resolution.* It had a singular fate, which we will consider with his other books later; it was never completed: Parsons was too much taken up with politics, action and controversy.

That autumn a long letter of advice to Mary Queen of Scots was intercepted and deciphered by the English government. It

1. Bess of Hardwick

2. Sir William Cavendish

GEORGIVS TALBOTVS
COMES SALOPIÆ
AN· ÆTATIS 58
S· H
1580

3. The Earl of Shrewsbury

P·ROBERTUS PERSONIUS ANGLUS
Soc·Iesu Socius et Superior P·Campiani in
pria Missione Anglicana: obiit 15·Ap·1610·Ætat suæ 64·
Ascendit ex adverso et opposuit murum pro domo Israel·Ezech·13

4.   Father Robert Parsons

5. Edward de Vere, 17th Earl of Oxford

6. Lord Chamberlain Hunsdon

7. Sir John Harington

9. Elizabeth I

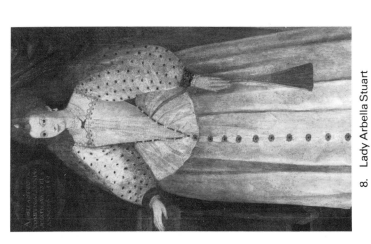

8. Lady Arbella Stuart

10. Lord Burghley

put forward a plan for her escape if Mary could be outside the house where she now lies, 'with one or two persons disguised about midnight . . . and so provide that it may be kept secret for two or three hours after – we doubt not so to provide for the rest that all England shall never take you again. If your Majesty can be brought to the seaside there shall be a vessel ready, sufficiently provided to brook the sea from England in what way so ever, if God say Amen.' Parsons now had much experience in providing for Channel crossings to and from the heretic isle, but God did not say Amen: by this time Mary was too closely guarded to make a getaway.

The Jesuit assures the Queen that she is now the principal hope of Philip II and the Prince of Parma – and he had the hardihood to hint that it would greatly help if she were to treat with Parma, evidently for marriage. Meanwhile, her willingness to fall in with their plans gave them much encouragement. All this came into the hands of the government, like her later connivance at Babington's plot to assassinate Elizabeth. At that juncture the stupid Mendoza was urging upon Philip that Babington should also kill the worst of the heretics – Cecil, Hunsdon, Knollys, Walsingham and Beale, Clerk of the Privy Council. Philip had known Cecil in England and minuted that he might be spared; as for the rest, well and good. But it was Mary whom the egregious young Babington ruined: the evidence brought her to the block before the Armada sailed, so that the Crusade for England was left without its candidate for the throne. This eventually led to trouble and acute conflict between the factions among the exiles.

The year 1585 saw the war between England and Spain wide open to the world. The assassination of William the Silent left the Dutch without a leader, and their cause nearly beaten by Spanish military strength under its ablest commander, the Prince of Parma. The English were forced to intervene or – the Netherlands subjugated – their turn would come next. Leicester was sent with a rather scratch army, himself an amateur as a general; his step-son, Philip Sidney, in his following – to be casually killed at Zutphen.

That spring Parsons moved to Flanders to concert measures with Allen in preparation for the greatest Enterprise, the conquest of England. Philip II had decided on Parma to carry out his scheme, instructing him to consult with Allen and Parsons, who became *persona grata* at Parma's headquarters, intimate with his secretary and his household. The Jesuit knew well how to deal with princes; his diplomatic gifts and knowledge of languages stood him in good stead and made him an indispensable tool.

In the autumn the couple journeyed to Rome to urge support of Philip's Enterprise on Pope Sixtus V (this remarkable old man did not believe in it and, in addition, was an admirer of Queen Elizabeth and Francis Drake). Allen remained in Rome for the rest of his life, Parsons until the disaster to the Armada was undeniable, when he betook himself to Spain to make himself useful there.

His three years in Rome were not wasted, he was full of work and schemes. He continued to direct the English mission, taking satisfaction in sending Garnet as Jesuit Superior. This Wykehamist lasted in the job for nearly twenty years, such was the intolerance of Elizabeth's government, which surely indeed could have run him to earth at any time if it chose to. Not until the Gunpowder Plot, which he knew of, was he laid by the heels by James I's government. Parsons acted as Latin secretary to the Jesuit General for a period, then took the place of Father Holt as Rector of the English College, when Allen dispatched him and Father Cresswell to Flanders to be in readiness for the Armada. Meanwhile Parsons' European correspondence continued. He worked at his edition of Sanders' venomous book on the English Schism, making large additions to it. In season and out of season he urged the reluctant Sixtus V to supply funds for Philip's vast Enterprise, and he lobbied incessantly for Allen to be made Cardinal in time for the Day of Judgment for England. In August 1587 he had his desire: Allen reported to Parma, 'next under heaven Father Parsons made me Cardinal'.

As the time of the Armada approached the new Cardinal

launched his Admonition to the English Nation, warning them of the wrath to come – a monstrous manifesto charging the Queen with her (questionable) bastardy, renewing her 'deposition' and releasing her subjects from their allegiance. Both Allen and Parsons were traitors; neither of them could ever show face in England again or he would have been hanged – and rightly. They must have been bitterly disappointed at the upshot of the Armada; but immediately Allen wished Parsons to go to Spain to urge Philip 'not to leave off so', but to continue in his godly purpose.

For most of the next nine years Parsons was in Spain, where he identified himself with Philip's purposes and was regarded with favour in consequence. In Spain he was safe – as he was not in France; for by this time he had incurred the hatred of his opponents among the exiles, notably the lay leaders in Paris, Charles Paget and Morgan. It was from this group that emanated the scurrilous *Leicester's Commonwealth*, charging him with all sorts of crimes, based – it was said – upon information largely supplied by the reptilian Lord Henry Howard. Parsons was now so notorious as the leading propagandist against his country that he has frequently been charged with this poisonous effusion too. He had no hand in it.

Arrived in Spain Parsons had an audience of the King about the business he had come on, and immediately set to work, with his organising ability, to take the English priests and students he found there under his wing – and under his orders. He wrote to Douai to send a contingent to Spain in case of disaster to the seminary in the encroaching war in the Netherlands. At Valladolid he found a group of exiles whom he proposed to take over and form into another seminary. The ecclesiastical authorities there, Spanish fanatics to a man, opposed a settlement from a country steeped in heresy, as liable to be infectious. That did not frustrate Father Robert: he procured an order from Court putting a stop to opposition. He hired a house, drafted the students into it, and put them under Jesuit discipline – thus began in 1589 the English College at Valladolid on the site it occupies to this day.

He managed to raise funds for it – he was a great fund-raiser –

more houses were bought and a chapel built. When one goes there, one sees its prime treasure: the Vulnerata – the mutilated statue of the Virgin which the philistine English soldiery dragged through the streets of Cadiz upon its capture in 1596. Now it occupies the place of honour above the high altar. In a couple of years the College was able to receive Parsons' nephew, John, from Rheims as a student. In the year of the capture of Cadiz he was sent on the English mission, which he happily survived to end up as a Carthusian at Malines after 1615.

We cannot go in detail into Parsons' incessant activities in Spain. From Valladolid he sent Father Flack to start a new seminary at St Omer, and arranged for the Jesuit Henry Walpole to succeed him. In 1592 he dispatched a group of students from Valladolid to form a seminary at Seville; a group of priests at neighbouring San Lucar he formed into a community under orders to expedite seminary priests to England. A similar community was organised at Madrid. It may be imagined that all this entailed much work and negotiation, journeyings about Spain, in which he once and again fell ill.

All the while his writing continued, a European correspondence of much importance, with Rome and the General of the Jesuits, works of propaganda and controversy. Though he had considerable hopes of the seminaries, over which he jockeyed himself into a position of general supervision and authority, he never ceased to urge political objectives. He wrote to Philip's Secretary of State, 'to think to get the upper hand in England without having a party within the realm is a great illusion. And to think to have this party without forming it and keeping it together is a great illusion.' *Verb. sap.* He worked consistently and ruthlessly towards that end; himself had no illusions except perhaps the illusion of hope. But then, as de Gaulle used to say, *'Pour agir il faut espérer'*.

The English government was well apprised of what Parsons was up to from some of his co-religionists. Father Cecil alias Snowden, for example, was one of those whom Parsons had drawn from Rheims to Valladolid, whence he sent the priest on the English mission. Taken prisoner, he reported Parsons' doings, without ceasing to be a Catholic: he remained one of the numerous secular priests who opposed the Jesuit line. He reported that Parsons had secured Philip's permission to send the first-fruits of his new seminary disguised as soldiers; that they were to assure English Catholics that Spain meant no conquest but only the reform of religion; while at the same time representing to Philip that the English Catholics were entirely at his devotion. 'They are enemies not only of the present state but of Catholics themselves, and by their practices abroad cause poor men to suffer at home. . . . Many Catholics at home and abroad dislike Allen and Parsons' proceedings in bringing foreign forces and potentates against their own country.' Another priest, one Dingley, thought that Parsons was the only man England need fear – he was constantly urging Spain on with his reports, arguments and persuasions.

In fact Father Cecil had been instructed to talk about the succession to the throne in England and to direct Catholics to look towards Lord Strange, of the Stanley family, Earls of Derby, who were crypto-Catholics. Their cousin Sir William Stanley – who was being considered for Lord Deputy of Ireland – had caused immense dismay in the Netherlands by treacherously betraying Deventer, of which he was governor, to the Spaniards; while his subordinate had betrayed the fort at Zutphen. They then went over to the Spaniards. Parsons had procured a pension of 3600 crowns from Philip for the traitor Stanley, who, discontented at not being employed, spent much of his time at the College at Valladolid. This last bit of information came from yet a third priest, John Fixer alias Thomas Wilson, who proved very well informed about the goings-on in Spain.

Nothing is more tedious than religious controversy, for it is mostly about non-sense issues, therefore self-proliferating and consequently interminable. We will then not tire the reader with Parsons' all too numerous writings in this field, having undergone the tedium of reading most of them. But we must except Parsons' positive work, which became well known under the title of *A Christian Directory* and went into many editions;

for it had the curious fate of being found useful by Anglicans, when pared of its Romanist accretions and suitably edited.

This job was performed by a Yorkshire clergyman, Edmund Bunny, in 'an eirenical spirit, hoping that well-willers would appreciate common ground' and deploring 'books of controversy engendering inordinate heat'. This was very Anglican of him, and also rather naïf; for controversy was just what Father Robert loved, and he was provoked to some heat in reply, found Bunny's unfortunate name funny, calling him 'Buny' all the way through.

Parsons' book had been suggested by that of a fellow Jesuit, Gaspar Loart, which decided him to write his own; since 'books of controversy help little to the good life, filling men's heads with the spirit of contention' – he 'misliked that men should spend so much time unprofitably'. Here was Satan rebuking sin! Bunny wrote that he had meant only to persuade 'those discontented countrymen of ours to more moderate ways and to better agreement in the cause of religion'; and so he had left all that he thought 'might tolerably stand', though he did reproach Father Robert with 'how confidently you are wont to speak on your own behalf'. Parsons was indignant at being made 'to speak like a good minister of England; in place of a priest hearing confessions, a minister giving counsel'. We may well ask, what difference did it make? It was rather a good joke that Bunny played on Father Robert, though he had not meant it in that spirit.

Parsons was a trained Oxford man, and his book built up the foundations of orthodox Christian belief from the proper philosophical presuppositions – Aristotle, Plato, St Thomas Aquinas; the *primum mobile*, the argument from the wonder of the world and its design; 'that there is a God which rewardeth good and evil'; that there is 'a final end and cause for which man was created by God and placed in this world' – the whole teleological scheme. A scientific spirit, a mere naturalist who described things as they are – like Francis Bacon – was condemned: Galen, for example, who dominated Renaissance medicine, was 'a profane and very irreligious physician'. And we know from another work Parsons' description of the most brilliant mathematician in England, Thomas Hariot, the instructor of Ralegh's circle: 'the conjuror that is master thereof, wherein both Moses and our Saviour, the Old and New Testaments, are jested at'. Parsons concluded that 'the service which God requireth of man in this present life is religion', as against 'the Love of this World'. Himself should know: we can hardly regard him as altogether unworldly.

Bunny had innocently hoped to deliver Catholics from the burdens of confession and penance, and vows of chastity and monkery, and invited them to be partakers of the state of Elizabethan England, 'never more prosperous'. He had even been so unwise as to say all might be members of one Catholic Church, though some were better members than others. This was insupportable – 'this is Mr Buny's good fellowship in religion!' The poor Bunny had said that to *insist* on division 'we bring ourselves to needless trouble'. Father Robert thought this very unreasonable – it is only fair to add, as would a good many others on both sides, who preferred killing each other for their mutually exclusive nonsense.

We need go no further into the matter, for Father Robert now had something more exciting in hand.

The execution of Mary Stuart had created an awkward problem for the English exiles: who was to succeed Queen Elizabeth? The great majority of Catholics at home had been loyal enough in spite of Popes' fulminations and Parsons' persuasions. The majority of secular Catholics in exile, especially those in Paris, looked to James of Scotland as the successor – but he was a Protestant, even a Calvinist (Queen Elizabeth had at least not been that). Parsons now addressed himself to the question with his usual alacrity and enthusiasm, his learning and plausibility, his more than normal facility for thinking up arguments to prove what he wished. In 1594, under the imprint of R. Doleman, he produced *A Conference about the Next Succession to the Crown of England*. This is sometimes taken seriously as a contribution to political theory; it created more of a stink than any other of his works and raised up yet more enemies in his own communion.

We may perhaps briefly traverse Parsons' arguments: 'that

succession to government by nearness of blood is not by law of nature or divine, but only by human and positive laws of every particular commonwealth, and consequently that it may *upon just causes* be altered by the same'. Supported by a learned array of authorities, this is obvious enough. There are particular forms of monarchies and different laws according as each commonwealth has chosen and established. But – some monarchs are lawfully chastised by commonwealths for misgovernment. Another monarch may 'justly be put back if he hath not the parts requisite'. Unobjectionable, we may agree. Then – 'how the next in succession by propinquity of blood have oftentimes been put back by the commonwealth and others further off admitted in their places'. 'What are the principal parts which a commonwealth ought to respect in admitting or excluding any prince?' Whether he is a Catholic is the answer. Q. E. D.

To his book Parsons appended a genealogy showing how Philip II's favourite daughter, the Infanta Isabella, was descended from John of Gaunt: she would make the most suitable successor to the throne of England. What had it got to do with him? But this was what people did say, both Catholics and Protestants. Sir John Hayward, in his reply[2] to the book said, 'What have you to do with reasons of state? Your office is to meditate, to pray, to instruct men in pure devotion, to settle their souls in piety and peace. But do you contain yourselves within these limits? Nothing less. You take upon you the policy of state; you rend and deface the policy of kings; you make yourselves both moderators and judges of all their actions.' So much for the Jesuit itch to intermeddle with matters of state.

The great majority of Catholics were as much affronted as were Protestants, perhaps even more so for they were endangered by it. We learn from a priest sent from Rome on mission in 1599 that 'Parsons propounded to have his book of Succession read in the English College'; and told this priest, Barnby, that 'he intended to meet with the Infanta and the Archduke at Milan upon their return, and would come along with her into the Low Countries'. Another instructed Catholic, angered by Jesuit policy, took up the argument. 'We were towards peace with our Prince: why doth he provoke her sword against innocents by bringing into the realm novelties, not only against the late Parliamental laws but also the fundamental Catholic laws of our country established three hundred years ago? . . . This other obtruded authority is conjoined with matters of state in the highest degree. What but their insolent challenge to the whole realm was the cause of all the hard laws and edicts made to the undoing and death of so many Catholics?'[3]

Dr Gifford, who became Archbishop of Rheims, wrote that 'Parsons seeks the simple monarchy of England *per fas et nefas*', and regarded his book as 'the most pestilent ever made: never anything was written which hath made such a broil'. The Papal Nuncio in Paris was angry with Parsons and at his book, and says that Parsons will never rise while the present Pope lives. Allen died this year, 1594, and the Jesuits at Rome wanted Parsons made cardinal. He never was.

The historian's interest in the matter is the intellectual one: why do these people never state the simple truth that they argue only what suits the position they take up on other grounds? Their 'arguments' are merely a smoke-screen for what they want. It gets rid of a great deal of human nonsense, and saves a lot of time and energy, to realise that; one need hardly ever pay much attention to what ordinary people suppose themselves to 'think'. But one need not suppose that a clever man like Parsons was unaware of what he was up to: he might, unlike most people, be aware of his own motives. How many other people did he take in? People are all too easily taken in: they have no intellectual defences – though sometimes they have common sense. For example, both Parsons and Hayward knew that Richard III had sinned in murdering his nephews; so did Lord Henry Howard, great-grandson of Richard's crony whom he made Duke of Norfolk: the truth came down in the family tradition. But ordinary people, though they do not know it, cannot think – and so are apt to be at the mercy of the plausible Parsonses of this world.

The succession was indeed a ticklish, a crucial, subject as Elizabeth grew old and people wondered what would happen when she died. Such a matter belonged to the *arcana imperii*: it was Essex's unpardonable offence that he tried to jockey himself into a position to dominate the succession. That was what he, unforgivably by the Queen, discussed with her most formidable rebel, Tyrone, at the Ford. The weathercock William Alabaster – who was actually converted to Catholicism during Essex's capture of Cadiz! – received a message from Parsons to deliver to Essex: if he would support the Infanta's title, Spain was able to maintain him in it, and he would be rewarded according to his merit. There followed a typical Parsons touch, 'for he was too great to live under any of his competitors'. All the seminarists whom he dispatched on the English mission he had sworn to support the Infanta's succession. An Italian saying at the time was that an *Inglese italianato* was a *diabolo incarnato*; perhaps the same might be said even more appositely of an Hispaniolised Englishman. Parsons was thoroughly Hispaniolised: he had sold himself to Spain.

An Englishman who had been imprisoned at San Lucar bore witness that, while he was at Seville, either Parsons or Father Walpole, when head of the English College there, came daily to persuade them to alter their religion. Three captains with others had been brought to the College to be reconciled, which they performed, except Captain Crosse, who was taken back to the Inquisition. The expatriates were still in hopes, for two further Armadas were sent against England in 1596 and 1597. Parsons did his part in the preparations, instructing his students at Valladolid and Seville; some thirty priests altogether were said to be stayed from the English mission, so as to come with the Armada. Alas, nothing came of either of them: each suffered heavy losses from storms in the Bay, the second disastrous losses off Finisterre, where many ships foundered. God – or perhaps the weather – was against them.

In hope of these Armadas Parsons was writing his 'Memorials', 'which might be proposed in the first Parliament and National Council of England after God of his mercy shall restore the same to the Catholic faith'. There was to be restitution of monastic property (some hopes!), though dispensations might be granted to nobles holding it – but these were to be granted by Jesuits only, for they would prevail, secular priests discountenanced. Even more important, the Inquisition would be introduced. It would have to be – it would be needed. Understandably these Memorials were not made public, but a copy came into the English government's hand – as almost everything of Father Robert's did. Later he presented a copy to the Infanta, who of course was to have no use for it.

Meanwhile, in the English College at Rome, conflict between the students and their Jesuit superiors broke out more bitterly than ever: only Father Robert's indispensable presence could bring about order in the nursery. Before he left for Rome, the lifelong exile from Queen Mary's time, Sir Francis Englefield, wrote to Philip urging his strong support for Parsons at Rome, 'knowing the hatred and aversion with which he is regarded by the Scottish and French factions' – to these he might have added the secular priests. Englefield asked the King for 'an express order to the ambassador at Rome to prevent his detention there', and provide for his safety. Thus protected, Parsons took up his final residence at Rome.

He became Rector of the English College and, with his prestige and authority, quelled the trouble-makers. Though not a cardinal, he was treated as if he were one and exercised an ascendancy throughout the English missions; after all, he knew more about them and had laboured harder for them than anyone alive. At Douai the head of the College was under a secret vow of obedience to him. Charles Paget recognised that Parsons had the backing of Spain and affirmed that the General of the Jesuits had given him authority in English affairs, to send or recall as he thought good. Parsons believed in discipline – his own; he was reported as saying that it was 'needful to know not only that a man is a Catholic but what kind of Catholic he is'.

The secular priests in England were anxious for the appointment of a bishop with the usual powers. Not so Father Robert: he procured the appointment of an archpriest to supervise them, one Blackwell, who was secretly sworn to consult the Jesuit Superior, Garnet, in all matters of gravity. The priests at home sent delegates to Rome to protest; they were strictly confined at the English College and then banished. Over thirty priests in England signed an appeal to the Pope, and more bitter controversy than ever broke out, aimed almost wholly at Parsons. He did not fail to reply, first with his suave *Brief Apology*, then more scurrilously with his *Manifestation of the Folly of Certain Calling Themselves Secular Priests*. He upheld the superiority of priests living in community under regular discipline, religious orders, i.e. like his own. The Society of Jesus was faultless in his eyes; certainly its achievements in his time – everywhere except in England – were remarkable.

Father Tierney, the early Victorian priest and chaplain to the Duke of Norfolk, who published much of this religious correspondence in his edition of Dodd's *Church History*, was shocked by Parsons' disingenuousness – far more flagrant even than Manning's treatment of Newman. At the moment when Father Robert asserted that he was sending out letters all 'for sweetness and moderation', he was publishing his *Manifestation*, in which the deputies from the seculars are 'assaulted with the most unmeasured abuse; and the very person who is here addressed in terms of friendship [Father Mush] is there sneered at as having been "a poor rude serving-man", received and educated in the English College out of charity and known afterwards by the appellation of Doctor Dodipoll Mush'. Parsons often found other people's names funny; his own would seem to indicate that fairly recently the family were the offspring of a parson – i.e. a celibate priest. It may be that this gave his enemies the idea that he was illegitimate – and also why his co-religionists are careful to spell him 'Persons' in their publications.

Again and again Father Tierney has a shocked note at the contrast between disingenuous letters and 'appalling accusations – so painful and at the same time so humbling to our nature that the mind instinctively turns from its contemplation'. For me it offers a typical enough example of human obtuseness in a clever man – no wonder Swift admired Parsons. In practically the same breath he could say opposite things. People are hardly ever capable of consistency in thought, but with Father Robert it was more a case of not letting his right hand know what his left was doing. Father Tierney comments naïvely on the gap between precept and example: 'it is painful to think that the man who could dictate the excellent advice contained in this letter should himself by his writings be among the foremost to act in opposition to it'. Pareto would find it merely corroborative of human 'thinking'; Father Robert was a flagrant example of it. We need set no store whatever by what he thought, it is the *gap* that is so revealing.

When Parsons came back to Rome he tried to interest the Pope in a scheme to marry the Infanta to a papal nephew. When this didn't work he proposed the papal nephew as a husband for Arbella Stuart, next heir after James of Scotland. We find him negotiating with Cardinal d'Ossat for French support for this bright idea. Turn and twist as Parsons might, King James succeeded peaceably to Elizabeth's throne – Robert Cecil was more than a match for Robert Parsons. At once we find Parsons assuring that prayers were offered in the seminaries that King James might become a Catholic; that the Pope was delighted with the King's book, the *Basilicon Doron*; he recounted his services for the King's sainted mother and for him abroad, and prayed pardon for his 'share in' the Book of Succession. In writing to the King he tried to explain away his opposition to his succession as 'mere feints to drive him to reconciliation with the Church'. By this time how many people, one wonders, were taken in by anything he said?

There came up the question of a new Oath of Allegiance. James, like Elizabeth before him, was far more tolerant towards Catholics than Parliament ever was, and a new oath was specially trimmed to meet Catholic susceptibilities and make it easier for them to affirm their loyalty to the King in secular matters, like other subjects. This was not good enough for Father Robert: he was a prime mover in getting the Papacy to forbid Catholics to take this moderate oath. The poor seminary priests in England had to labour on under the threat of imprisonment, riveted on their necks by no one, under God, more than Parsons. He expressed regret that even the Archpriest Blackwell and the prisoners in the Clink 'do persist in their erroneous opinions about the Oath' – let us note, as Pareto would, that 'erroneous' means what Parsons did not agree with.

Let us also cite a characteristic example of his disingenuous style. Writing of himself in the third person, under an assumed name, he assures a correspondent that he has abstained from dealing with the affairs of the secular priests. 'Yet, being in the place he is, when he is asked his opinion, he cannot but speak it, with his reasons for the same. And this for as much concerneth only the public, wherein he cannot but think he hath as much interest as another to speak his mind. And those that are or will be angry for this must have patience with him, as he hath with them.' And so on. It sounds so plausible – and one cannot but join Swift in admiring Parsons' prose style: nothing of the turgidness of so many Elizabethan writers about it.

Father Tierney is shocked to catch him out lying: the whole scheme of the archpriest originated with him – while 'professing as I do that neither I have nor desire to have any least part in the managing of their affairs'. We must allow that he had a genius for managing. Then, 'for my own part, I have borne myself towards them as though I had been their scholar and they brought me up, and not I them; and as if they were ancient men in this Court [Rome] and knew all things that were to be done, and I were young and knew nothing'. Do we detect a note of spiritual pride, the worst of sins to a Catholic? Perhaps we may detect a justified sense of intellectual superiority, along with his pride at being in the know.

After all, there were few who could confront on an equal intellectual level the government's defender of the Oath and the Royal Supremacy, the redoubtable Attorney-General Coke. Parsons threw himself into the fray impetuously as usual – but he had behind him the authority of the eminent Jesuit scholar Cardinal Bellarmine. Again we need hardly traverse in detail the theoretical question at issue[4] – whether the Act of Supremacy and authority to execute jurisdiction in religious matters conformed to the ancient laws of England, and so were merely declaratory, as Coke argued; or no, as Parsons argued. Parsons had a good intellectual case, and on the whole past history was with him. But what of it? Power was what mattered, and the consensus of the nation; and the nation had decided.

The prospects for wider toleration had been dealt a deadly

blow by the idiocy of Gunpowder Plot, and it brought the
Jesuit Superior, Garnet – who had happily survived some
twenty years – to the block. In the course of his examination he
admitted that Parsons had written to him asking what plots
were now afoot, but that he had left the letter unanswered.
Unwise as usual – when it would have been wiser to shut up in
such a case – Parsons went bull-headed to the charge: it was
unfair to blame the Society of Jesus for the Gunpowder treason,
'when only one or two at most heard in confession what they
could not avoid'. But they could have found means of heading
it off, as the crypto-Catholic Lord Henry Howard, now promoted Earl of Northampton and a leading member of James's
government, insisted at the examination of the plotters: he said
outright that he should have been tipped off.

Nor did Parsons hesitate to defend the Jesuit doctrine of
equivocation which made such a bad impression at Garnet's
trial. He replied to Coke: 'it hath not been, I think, your education to be troubled much with scrupulosity of words: to wit,
what sense may be held therein without sin, and what not'.
True enough: though Coke was a lawyer, he was no casuist.
'The examination of which matters belongs more to tender and
timorous consciences than Kings' Attorneys commonly are
presumed to have, who must speak to the purpose, howsoever
it be to the truth.' No one would suppose Coke to have a tender
and timorous conscience: would anyone suppose Parsons to be
any better? Each, of course, was convinced that he had hold of
the truth, i.e. his own opinion. We need go no further into the
matter.

Defeated in all his political schemes, frustrated on every front,
Parsons flung himself in his last years more than ever into controversy. Having made himself a prime target, he was bent on
answering everybody back – not only Attorney-General Coke,
but Sir Francis Hastings, Bishop Morton, Bishop Barlow,
Matthew Sutcliffe, even the insignificant Thomas Bell: it was
irresistible to write *The Doleful Knell of Thomas Bell*. When one
reads even a tithe of these books and pamphlets flying to and

fro, one wonders whether Father Robert was quite right in the
head. Certainly he became increasingly unpopular with Pope
Clement VIII, on account of his constantly stirring up controversy. The Jesuit General suggested a convenient retirement
to Naples, until the Pope's death. After that, Father Robert,
irrepressible as ever, returned to Rome to be confirmed as pre-
fect of the missions by the General: he seems never to have put a
foot wrong with the Society with which he had identified himself and which had brought him European fame.

From what few traces remain in the records he had dragged
his family along in his wake. In 1598 a brother of his surfaced at
St Omer, married to an English gentlewoman. In 1599 an
informer reported a kinsman who had been engaged for the past
three years in conveying Catholics and intelligence to and fro
across Channel. We have already noted nephew John, whom
uncle Robert summoned from Rheims to Spain and thence to
the English mission. In August 1599 another nephew, Thomas,
popped up who had served twenty years in Spain: he came as a
Frenchman in a French ship to Mount's Bay, where he was
examined by a local J. P. Nephew Thomas 'counterfeited fool'
and so got away to his ship – an authentic Parsons touch.

We may leave the last word on the issue to a man of genius,
no less than John Donne, from his work the *Pseudo-Martyr*.[5]
This work is mistakenly little read by literary scholars, though
it is Donne's most important prose-work and of acute historical
significance. Donne had been brought up in Parsons' doctrines,
for his family was ultramontane Catholic and had suffered in
consequence: two of his Heywood uncles, ex-Fellows of All
Souls, had been Jesuits in and out of prison; his mother's family
belonged to the Rastells also, exiles in Louvain, and thus related
to the grand martyr, St Thomas More.

It took Donne a long time to think himself clear from these
influences upon his youth. 'I had a longer work to do than
many other men; for I was first to blot out certain impressions
of the Roman religion and some anticipations early laid upon
my conscience: both by persons who by nature had a power and
superiority over my will and others who, by their learning and
good life, seemed to me justly to claim an interest for the guid-

ing and rectifying of mine understanding in these matters.' Now for some years he had given himself to studying the whole issue of the conflict between Rome and England, reading up the authorities and thinking things out for himself. In particular, the cult of martyrdom and the insistence upon making martyrs. 'I have ever been kept awake in a meditation of martyrdom, by being derived from such a stock and race as, I believe, no family which is not of far larger extent and greater branches hath endured and suffered for obeying the teachers of Roman doctrine than it hath done.'

Were their sacrifices necessary, in particular the sacrifice of life? Donne at once allows that 'if priests confined themselves to their spiritual functions, to die for that were martyrdom'. But 'refusing the oath of allegiance vitiates the integrity of the whole act', and robs them of martyrdom: they are pseudo-martyrs. Donne proceeds to go into the issue with scrupulousness and learning. Parsons had laid it down that refusing the Oath of Allegiance was a matter of faith. Donne showed from all the authorities that 'the doctrine itself is not certain, nor presented as a matter of faith'; that, if Bellarmine argued for it, he varied in his statements of it and was contradicted by Catholics of equal estimation.

On the practical side: nothing in the Oath violated the Pope's *spiritual* jurisdiction. France and Venice had always maintained their just laws for temporal jurisdiction, 'which laws Parsons, without any colour of truth or escape from malicious and gross deceiving, says they have recalled'. This is not true, Donne says, compare Parsons' own *Relation*. All the English king requires is shown in the kings of France, not by virtue of any concordat but by the inherent right of the Crown; nothing can give the Pope any more right over England than over any other free state. In fact the whole course from the Bull of Deposition and Excommunication of 1570 had been a terrible mistake – as it was. Philip of Spain had rejected all attempts of the Pope to interpose between Spain and Portugal – contrary to what Parsons says, 'who is no longer a subject and son of the Church of Rome than as that Church is an enemy of England, for in the differences between her and Spain he abandons her'.

Donne does not say so, but it cannot have escaped his pen-
etrating psychological perception that revenge upon England
had entered strongly into Parsons' motives. One can understand
it, in a way sympathise with it: for a man of genius to be rejected
is not nice, as Swift understood.

And so Father Robert had driven scores, superfluously, to
their deaths. Donne understood the psychology of priests ready
to be martyred, to which the insinuating Jesuit could appeal:
'carried to this desire by human respects, and by the spirit either
of their blood and parents when they do it to please them; or by
the spirit of giddiness and levity; or by the spirit of liberty, to be
delivered from the bondage and encumbrances of wife and children; or else violently by adversity and want'. All this and
more entered into it; he does not mention camaraderie, the
support and encouragement of one's fellows, bravado and pride
making it impossible to yield.

'It becomes not me to say that the Roman religion begets
treason, but I may say that, within one generation, it degener-
ates into it.' The outstanding figure of that generation was
Robert Parsons, and Donne points the finger unerringly to his
responsibility in his description of him as 'an ordinary instrument of his [the Devil], whose continual libels and incitatory
books have occasioned more afflictions and drawn more of that
blood which they call Catholic in this kingdom than all our
Acts of Parliament have done'.

We have a last, rather sad close-up of the famous, inflamma-
tory Jesuit from a report of him in the last couple of years left to
him. With the Jacobean peace it was possible for English visitors once more to visit Rome, though a careful watch was kept
on them by the Inquisition. In February 1609 Simon Willis
reported on his visit, along with Sir Robert Chamberlain and
Sir Edmund Hampden. They were there to see the sights of the
city and its antiquities, but they addressed themselves to the
Jesuit Nicholas Fitzherbert for advice how to conduct themselves. 'Albeit there hath been many years a mortal hatred between Mr Fitzherbert and Parsons, yet did Mr Fitzherbert advise
us to afford him a complimental visitation, thereby to restrain
him from informing against us to the Inquisitors.

'We therefore went to the [English] College to see him, but

were answered the first day that he was in physic. The next day we went again, and were then admitted to his chamber. He asked our names, and whether we were of Oxford or Cambridge; and having been answered by the two knights – to whom he addressed his speech – that we had been of Oxford, he presently [i.e. immediately] fell into a discourse of the difference between our universities and the universities of foreign parts where he had lived, commending the order and method of the study of the foreign before ours.' Typical Parsons: whether true or no, that was the line he would take – against his own country to the end. 'With which discourse he entertained us a quarter of an hour or thereabouts without demanding us of our religion or any other matter whatsoever.

'Then he offered to show us the house, and led us first into the library, which was poor and scarce worthy that name. From thence into their refectory, as mean as the former; and, for aught we saw, all the house in general so mean as not to be compared with the meanest hall in Oxford. He then took leave of us, using only these speeches: "Gentlemen, I shall desire you one day, before you leave the town, to come and do penance with us by taking a bad dinner: which is all the courtesy this poor house can afford our countrymen." Howbeit, he never invited us, neither did any of us ever see him afterwards.'[6]

Does one detect a note of disillusionment and defeat after a lifetime of such prodigious efforts to reverse the way in which England was set? One observes a similar reaction in the last days of Cardinal Allen at Rome – a conciliatory kindness to visiting English – after the joint endeavours of Allen and Parsons to bring about the defeat of their country at the hands of Spain. They were obliged at length to recognise their own defeat.

It was not long before the famous Jesuit died, after a short illness, on 15 April 1610. But what a prodigious career Father Robert made for himself after ceasing to be a Fellow of Balliol! He was buried, at his request, in the chapel of the English College beside Cardinal Allen, with whom he had laboured so valiantly for what they supposed the good of their native country.

SOURCES In addition to books mentioned in the text and notes, the *Calendars of State Papers Domestic; Letters and Memorials of Father Robert Persons*, I, ed. L. Hicks, Catholic Record Society, vol. 39; *The English College at Valladolid*, Registers, ed. E. Henson, Catholic Record Society, vol. 30; *The Liber Ruber of the English College at Rome*, ed. W. Kelly, Catholic Record Society, vol. 37; *The First and Second Diaries of the English College, Douay*, ed. T. F. Knox; *Dodd's Church History of England*, ed. M. A. Tierney.

3

Edward de Vere, 17th Earl of Oxford

HE 17th Earl of Oxford was, as the numbering shows, immensely aristocratic, and this was the clue to his career. In Elizabethan society full of new and upcoming men, some of them at the very top, like the Bacons and Cecils – the Boleyns themselves, from whom the Queen descended, were a new family – the Oxford earldom stood out as the oldest in the land. He was the premier earl and, as hereditary Lord Great Chamberlain, took place on the right hand of the Queen and bore the sword of state before her. This office went right back to his ancestor, the first Earl, Aubrey de Vere, upon whom Henry I conferred it in 1133; it must be distinguished from that of the Lord Chamberlain of the Household, who had a great deal of actual work to do. The office of Lord Great Chamberlain of England had become purely honorific and came alive only on grand ceremonial occasions, such as coronations, feasts of the Order of the Garter, and thanksgivings.

The Veres went back to earliest Norman times, and continued to occupy their splendid Norman keep at Castle Hedingham – which still exists, a fine ruin – in the Colne valley on the fertile borders of Essex and Suffolk. They founded the priory of Earls Colne, where generations of them were buried. With the Reformation the church became a ruin, and such of the

75

Vere monuments as remained were removed in our time to the parish church of Bures not far away.

Of this old medieval family we still remember the 9th Earl, Richard II's favourite, whom he made Duke of Ireland. Exiled by the Merciless Parliament in 1388, Vere was killed while hunting in the Netherlands by a boar – strangely enough, the family crest was a boar. When the embalmed body was brought home the cypress coffin was opened so that Richard could gaze once more upon the beloved face and clasp the hand of his friend.

The Tudors owed a debt of gratitude to the 13th Earl, who kept the flame of loyalty to the Lancastrian house alight through all the bad days for them of the Yorkist ascendancy, and commanded Henry Tudor's forces at Bosworth.

All these things had their importance for Elizabeth, who was socially more conservative than her father. His two great ministers were – one, Wolsey, son of an unrespectable Ipswich butcher; the other, Cromwell, son of a Putney brewer who was really a Welsh Williams. Even Bacons were more respectable than that. Naunton noted that 'the Queen in her choice never took into her favour a mere new man or a mechanic'. She was particularly careful to preserve the peerage: she would not allow young peers who had not yet equipped themselves with an heir to serve abroad. She had frightful difficulty in making up her mind to the execution of her only duke, Norfolk.

Other people followed suit in their marked deference to an earl of the oldest historic family. It largely accounts for the endless patience and forbearance with which the Queen and Burghley treated the divagatory course of the gifted, neurotic, unstable 17th Earl, and the sycophancy with which he was treated by followers and those who hoped for his patronage.

It looks as if most young Elizabethan aristocrats were spoiled – perhaps not unnaturally those who had lost their fathers early and were royal wards. It was true both of Essex and Southampton, hardly less so of Rutland and young Lord Herbert – and most of all was it true of the 17th Earl of Oxford. The boy's father was an extravagant, easy-going fellow who had borne the crown at Anne Boleyn's coronation. He had married first a

Neville, of that famous family with whom the Veres had inter-married before; but, secondly, a local girl, Margaret Golding. Her half-brother, Arthur Golding, was the most prolific of early Tudor translators, making available in English classical authors and thousands of pages of the indigestible Calvin.

The father died in 1562, when Edward was only twelve. At once the new Earl came riding out of Essex from the grand funeral into the City, 'with seven score horse all in black' – an extravagant display even for that time. As a royal ward he was taken into that school of virtue, Cecil House in the Strand – Sir William was not yet Lord Burghley and the four-turreted house with its fine garden was only just finished. Here, under the surveyance of the great man, Edward was placed under the direction of a succession of distinguished tutors: for the first couple of years his uncle Golding; then the remarkable scholar, Laurence Nowell; for a time, the no less scholarly Sir Thomas Smith. Young Oxford was sent only briefly to St John's Col-lege, Cambridge – Burghley's own; but he emerged from this training well educated, with literary interests and of good promise, considering that along with his rank.

In 1564 Golding dedicated to his nephew his version of a Renaissance favourite, *Trogus Pompeius*, in the hope that Epaminondas and other classic heroes 'will encourage you to proceed in learning and virtue, and yourself thereby become equal to any of your predecessors in advancing the honour of your noble house'. We hear that note sounded again and again in the youth's ears – and we shall see how it worked out. Next year, Golding published his translation of Ovid's *Metamor-phoses*, the poet who most of all influenced Elizabethan poets and dramatists; with its unsuitable amorous and amoral stories it was not dedicated to the young Earl, but more appropriately to the Earl of Leicester, who, for all his Puritan patronage, knew all about such things.

In dedicating his translation of Calvin's *Commentaries on the Psalms* to his nephew, now twenty-one, Golding strikes, in 1571, a more dubious note. He adjured Oxford 'to consider how God has placed you upon a high stage in the eyes of all men. If your virtue be not counterfeit, if your religion be sound and pure, if your doings be according to true godliness, you shall be a stay to your country and an increase of honour to your house. But if you should become either a counterfeit Protestant or a professed Papist, or a cool and careless neuter (which God forbid), the harm could not be expressed which you should do to your native country.' The uncle does not 'mistrust' his nephew – but mistrust is precisely what the passage breathes, and what the young Earl was to merit, richly and continually, by his conduct.

In 1567 Oxford was admitted to Burghley's Inn of Court, Gray's Inn, at the same time as another promising youth, Philip Sidney. But that summer, Oxford's guardian noted in his Diary: 'Thomas Brinknell, an under-cook, was hurt by the Earl of Oxford at Cecil House, whereof he died; and by a verdict found *felo-de-se* with running upon a point of a fence-sword of the said Earl's.' Juries were inclined to be generous towards gentlemen who were under-age, to whom such accidents happened; but it was Cecil who got his ward off, as a note in his Diary records: 'I did my best to have the Jury find the death of a poor man whom he killed in my house to be found *se defendendo* [i.e. in defending himself].'

A memorandum of the youth's expenses for apparel, with rapiers and daggers, for the four years to 1566 amounts to £627. 15s. In gorgeous display at Court men were apt to wear 'whole manors on their backs'; for this youth we find yards of velvet and satin, taffeta and velvet hats, plumes of feathers, garters with silver ends, sheets of fine holland and handkerchiefs of cambric, with ten pairs of Spanish leather shoes for one quarter alone. But along with this are bought a Chaucer, Plutarch's works in French – Amyot's translation, from which Sir Thomas North made his – Cicero and Plato's works in folio, a Geneva Bible, and two Italian books. The young Lord was a reader.

In 1569 Thomas Underdowne was dedicating his translation of Heliodorus' *Aethiopian History*, in interesting terms: in 'matters of learning a nobleman ought to have a sight, but to be too much addicted that way I think it is not good'. However, 'such virtues be in your honour, such haughty courage joined with great skill, such sufficiency in learning, so good nature and common sense that in your honour is, I think, expressed the right pattern of a noble gentleman'. Such were the terms with which expectant authors addressed noble patrons – and received their reward if accepted. Oxford accepted many dedications, and received at least two authors into his service for a time – John Lyly and Anthony Munday. His promise was recognised; his 'conspicuous consumption' greater. When his period of wardship was over and he attained his majority, he came riding into London 'to his house by London Stone, with four score gentlemen in a livery of Reading tawny and chains of gold about their necks, before him; and one hundred tall yeomen in the like livery to follow him, without chains, but all having his cognizance of the Blue Boar embroidered on their left shoulder'. It must have cost a mint of money.

So too did tilts and tournaments at Court. In Maytime 1571 the young Earl had a success: 'Lord Oxford has performed his challenge at tilt, tourn and barriers – far above expectation of the world, and not much inferior to the other challengers. Their furniture was very fair and costly. The Earl's livery was crimson velvet, very costly. He himself and the furniture were in some more colours, yet he was the Red Knight.' Sir Henry Lee was the Green Knight, Charles Howard the White Knight, Christopher Hatton the Black Knight. Thus was the medieval world of chivalry conjured up in Elizabeth's England; such was Renaissance spectacle at her Court. All four challengers received a prize from her; she was much pleased by the young man's performance and awarded him a tablet of diamonds.

The next thing we hear of him that summer is that 'the Earl of Oxford hath gotten him a wife, or at the least a wife hath caught him. This is Mistress Anne Cecil, whereunto the Queen hath given her consent and the which hath caused great weeping and sorrowful cheer of those that had hoped to have that golden day.' It is fairly clear that this was a love match on Anne's part, and that she had caught the Earl. Her father was glad enough to marry his children into the grandest houses available, but one detects a note of dubiety under the honour he expressed at this consummation. There had been talk earlier of a

marriage with Philip Sidney – who was less attractive physi-
cally than Oxford. Evidently the young lady had made up her
mind to the bed she was to lie on.

One may infer from her father's letter that he would have
preferred another of his wards, the Earl of Rutland, to whom he
wrote: 'I think it doth seem strange to your lordship to hear of a
purposed determination in my Lord of Oxford to marry with
my daughter. And so, before his lordship moved it to me, I
might have thought it, if any other had moved it to me but
himself. For at his own motion I could not well imagine what to
think, considering I never meant to seek it nor hoped of it. And
yet reason moved me to think well of my Lord, and to acknowledge myself greatly beholden to him, as indeed I do.'

For a daughter of a mere knight, however important an official, this was a great match, and Cecil was sensible of the honour. Yet the note of doubt remains, as if he wishes to re-assure
himself: 'and surely, my lord, by dealing with him I find that
there is much more in him of understanding than any stranger
to him would think. And for mine own part I find that whereof
I take comfort in his wit and knowledge grown by good con-
versation.' An Elizabethan meant by 'wit' intelligence; evidently something else was wanting: nothing was said about
character, judgment or morals.

The marriage went ahead: nothing could be urged against it;
the Queen approved. The Earl was of age, over twenty-one,
Anne an innocent fifteen; the wedding took place in the week
before Christmas, 1571, with the Queen present. A grand feast
followed at Cecil House, at which everybody who was anybody was present. Cecil himself was up to his eyes in unravel-
ling the Ridolfi plot and the treasonable correspondence of
Norfolk now in the Tower. More than anyone Cecil was responsible for Norfolk's execution, and he had Parliament with him.
This displeased his new son-in-law, whose sympathies, like
those of other aristocrats, were with the Duke, head of their
order. The marriage began with no very happy augury.

Later on a rumour ran that the young Earl laid a ship to
convey the Duke abroad – but he was held too fast in the Tower
to make a get-away. Cecil won through the crisis by 1572,

emerging as Lord Burghley, the most powerful man in the kingdom. Oxford came round, though clearly there had been recriminations, for he wrote from his country place at Wivenhoe: 'I hope now to be more plausible unto you than heretofore, through my careful deeds to please you, which hardly – either through my youth or rather my misfortune – hitherto I have done.' He hoped that his 'backfriends' would not 'again undo your lordship's beginnings of well meaning of me . . . lest I, growing so slowly into your good opinion, may be undeservedly of my part voted out of your favour'. Evidently he had not Burghley's good opinion, 'to which I do aspire – though perhaps, by reason of my youth, your graver and severer years will not judge the same'.

This is the note which he will strike again and again – appeals to his youth to excuse his vagaries, his intemperance and misconduct. It is not a nice note.

However, at Court he was taken up and made much of by the Queen. This needs no explaining: an old maid now verging on forty, she had always liked the company of young men who combined good looks, a handsome person, with education and intelligence – Leicester and Hatton, later on there would be Ralegh and Essex. Now there was Oxford. In Maytime 1573 we learn that he 'is lately grown into great credit, for the Queen's Majesty delighteth more in his personage and his dancing and valiantness than any other. If it were not for his fickle head, he would pass any of them shortly. My Lady Burghley, unwisely, has declared herself, as it were, jealous [i.e. mistrustful, for her daughter's sake]: which is come to the Queen's ear, whereat she has been not a little offended with her, but now she is reconciled again. At all these love matters my Lord Treasurer [Burghley] winketh and will not meddle in any way.' He, 'even after the old manner, dealeth with matters of the state only, and beareth himself very uprightly'.

All round the Queen the Court talked and wrote and sang and danced the language of love; so far as she was concerned it was platonic love, and nobody was supposed to do anything about it. Ordinary flesh and blood couldn't stand it, in the constant contiguity of spirited young men and vulnerable maids-of-honour. Accidents happened, which invariably vexed the jealous Virgin deity.

The next thing was that Oxford absconded abroad. This was a serious offence: no one was allowed to leave the country without permission – as in Russia today, four hundred years later – and especially a leading Court figure, who might be going to join the political and religious exiles gathered in the Netherlands. There was something schizophrenic about Oxford; he was clearly torn in sympathies between his own aristocratic order, and the new deal incarnate in his father-in-law. The fear was that he might join the exiles; the Queen sent a messenger hot-foot after him, evidently with promises and assurances, for hot-foot he came back again.

This was the defence that was made of his venture. Walsingham assured Burghley that the Queen 'conceiveth great hope of his return, upon some secret message sent him'. Burghley was informed that the exiles – Oxford's Neville cousin Westmorland in particular – had hopes of him. But the Earl was back before the exiles were able to corral him: this enabled Burghley to defend him: 'howsoever my Lord of Oxford be, for his own part, in matters of thrift inconsiderate, I dare avow him to be resolute in dutifulness to the Queen and his country'. The Chancellor of the Exchequer, Sir Walter Mildmay, trusted that 'this little journey will make him love home the better hereafter. It were a great pity he should not go straight, there be so many good things in him to serve his God and Prince.'

We are beginning to see what these grave men of affairs thought of the promising young Earl: well educated, spirited, yet unstable, a 'fickle head'. Elizabeth, whose nicknames for her courtiers hit off their characters very well, called Oxford her 'Turk', where Burghley was her 'Spirit' – the brains of her administration.

It was only natural that the young Earl should wish to travel abroad: most leading Elizabethans made what came to be known in the eighteenth century as 'the grand tour'. In the sixteenth century it was important for those who were going to occupy place in a backward but up-and-coming country to equip themselves by foreign travel and observations abroad. There were risks and dangers, however, to health, purse, and morals. Such strait-laced Protestants as Burghley and Roger Ascham, Elizabeth's tutor, feared the impact of Italianate sophistication upon the morals, particularly the sexual morals, of innocent English youth. Yet Oxford's contemporary Philip Sidney had spent some years abroad without any harm coming to him, and he made most valuable contacts.

It is likely enough that Oxford was already chafing at the burdens and boredom of matrimony, for we note a certain pathos in a request of his young wife to Lord Chamberlain Sussex, on the Court coming to Hampton Court, that he would increase their lodging to three chambers, 'for the more commodious my lodging is the willinger, I hope, my Lord my husband will be to come thither'. But before he left Hampton Court for abroad he was heard to say that, if his wife had a child in his absence, it would be none of his.

He was already heavily in debt, to the tune of £6000, he estimated, so probably more. Burghley, knowing too well his profligacy, made what arrangements he could to protect his family. Oxford assigned some £3000 a year for his wife's living expenses and £666. 6s. 8d. for her jointure; for his sister, Lady Mary Vere, a mere £100. He estimated that he would require £1000 while overseas; in the event he spent the enormous sum of over £3700. It was obvious that sales of land would be necessary, and he left Burghley – who had plenty of other things to think of – with the responsibility for arranging them. Most of Oxford's letters from abroad are requests for money and more money, complaints that it was not forthcoming speedily enough or in sufficient amounts. He complained that he had left Burghley with authority to sell land as he thought fittest; the conscientious Lord Treasurer minuted beside this 'No such authority.' Recriminations followed, and one observes the tone of the letters waxing sour.

To begin with, the young man glad to be quit, all was well. He took the news that his wife was expecting their first child in good spirit, and from Paris sent her his picture and two horses.

At Strasbourg he visited the famous Sturmius, the educator of Protestant Europe, under whom Robert Sidney had studied, and then went on to Genoa and Venice, where he was ill for a while from fever and hurt his knee in a galley. He wrote home, rather querulously, in reply to his father-in-law's questions: 'for my liking of Italy, my Lord, I am glad I have seen it, and I care not ever to see it any more, unless it may be to serve my Prince and country'. That may be as it may be. He hoped that the money from the sale of his land had come in.

He was selling the whole of his inheritance in Cornwall and urged that 'that first order for mine expenses in this travel be gone through and withal. And to stop my creditors' exclamations – or, rather, defamations I may call them – I shall desire your lordship. . . .' The next letter was an ultimatum to his father-in-law. 'Till I can better settle myself at home I have determined to continue my travel: the which thing in no wise I desire your lordship to hinder, unless you would have it thus: *ut nulla sit inter nos amicitia* [that there be no friendship between us]. For, having made an end of all hope to help myself by her Majesty's service – considering that my youth is objected to me, and for every step of mine a block is found to be laid in my way – I see it is but vain *calcitrare contra li busse* [to kick against the pricks].'

We see here a man not only with a grievance – unreasonable in itself, for he was not qualified for office – but with a complex against the Cecils, his father- and mother-in-law and his wife. He had talked light-headedly of going on to Constantinople and Greece, which few ever did; but further licence for travel was not available and he came home in a state of settled rage, to turn his back on wife and child, create misery for them and the family, and an appalling scandal.

Oxford was aided and abetted, and pretty certainly egged on, by Lord Henry Howard, brother of the late Duke of Norfolk. The only thing to be said for this creature was that he was a conservative; a much cleverer man, he had urged on his brother to the fatal entanglement with Mary Queen of Scots, over which Lord Harry himself saw the inside of the Tower, and not for the last time.[1] He suffered from frustrated ambition; scholarly and learned, disingenuous, insinuating, for ever intriguing; crypto-Catholic and crypto-homosexual, he did not come into his own until the sympathetic James came to the throne. He was inspired by mortal hatred for Burghley who had brought Norfolk and himself down, and was ready to injure him in any way that was surreptitious and secret. Here was his chance. Later, when Oxford saw through him – it took people some time to see through Lord Harry's schemes – he described him as the vilest of men.

On his arrival back in England Oxford affected to believe that the child born to his wife was not his. Anne had made her choice of a husband and she seems always to have loved him – presumably he had a lovable side, though he treated her for some years like a cad. Virtuous and naïve as she was – she was still only twenty – no one believed but that she was innocent and that her child was his. He would not make an open charge, which, in some ways, would be less cruel for it could be disproved; meanwhile, he not only refused to see her but declined to come to Court if she should be there. This blew the scandal wide open.

Burghley expostulated again and again, wrote endless letters reasoning with him, going into his complaints – but, of course, the Earl was not a man to reason with, nor indeed open to reason. He answered his father-in-law: 'I must let your lordship understand this much, that is, until I can better satisfy or advertise myself of some mislikes, I am not determined, as touching my wife, to accompany her. What they are – because some are not to be spoken of or written upon as imperfections – I will not deal withal. Some that otherwise discontented me I will not blazon or publish until it please me. And, last of all, I mean not to weary my life any more with such troubles and molestations as I have endured; nor will I, to please your lordship only, discontent myself.'

A lofty letter from a son-in-law to the greatest personage in the realm under the Queen; and utterly selfish, of course. Burghley, though greatly grieved, treated it all with his extraordinary patience, his customary show of meekness, even humility. Perhaps this aggravated the young man's dislike the more. It is a

curious thing that all Burghley's aristocratic wards reacted
against the great man – Oxford, Southampton, Rutland in turn.
What was it that so irritated them? A middle-class tone of self-
righteousness? Not only virtue, but the insistence upon it; a
show of humility covering the tracks of a very quick brain, so
that he was never at a loss, never caught out; a certain coolness,
an utter lack of passion; such inhuman correctness of judgment
– he always was right. It was intolerable. It certainly formed a
complex in these spoiled young lords, conscious of their rank
and social superiority – but finding their political and intellectual inferiority when they came up against him.

Since Oxford refused to receive his wife Burghley had to take
her and her child back to live with him. The husband wrote a
cruel letter that 'it doth very well content me; for there, as your
daughter or her mother's [Oxford disliked his strong-minded
mother-in-law, who wished him dead], more than my wife,
you may take comfort of her. And I, rid of the cumber thereby,
shall remain well eased of many griefs. I do not doubt but that
she hath sufficient proportion for her being to live upon and to
maintain herself.'

Here was the rub: Burghley was both rich and powerful. But
he couldn't do everything with the Queen, very much a power
on her own, the source of all gifts and grants. Not everything is
said in this long and tedious correspondence, but it is obvious
that Oxford wanted employment. It is also obvious to any
impartial observer, as it was to the Queen, that he was not fit
for a serious charge. Burghley said that he had tried to get him
made Master of the Horse, but he had been unable to prevail.
He took his grief to the Queen in an immensely long, rather
distracted, letter. Elizabeth knew very well what to think of
Oxford and, kindly as usual, was willing to help: not a post, but
next year Oxford was given the considerable *douceur* of the
manor of Rising, which had belonged to Norfolk, and so much
land as to make it worth £250 a year. This was a very considerable gift: no one has been able to make out why, or for what. I
think we may guess: a bribe.

The Earl was now willing to compromise: his wife might
return to Court, provided that he did not have to accompany

her or meet her there. In this year a further matrimonial trouble raised its head. The son of the virtuous and decidedly Protestant Duchess of Suffolk, Peregrine Bertie, had fallen in love with Oxford's sister, Lady Mary Vere, and was determined to marry her. The Duchess was highly displeased, and confided her troubles to Burghley – who had to hear so many. She had told the young woman plainly that she had rather her son matched anywhere else and why: 'our religions agree not, and . . . if she should prove like her brother, if an empire follows her I should be sorry to match so. She said that she could not rule her brother's tongue, nor help the rest of his faults. . . . I told her her brother used you and your daughter so evil that I could not require you to deal in it.'

We see what other people thought of the Earl and his conduct. Peregrine Bertie insisted on marrying the sister. It turned out unhappily.

Oxford returned to Court, bringing his new Italian fashions with him. Stow tells us that until then English milliners and haberdashers were not up in Continental fashions of embroidered gloves and girdles, trimmed with gold or silk, or with sophisticated washes and perfumes. Then Oxford brought from Italy 'gloves, sweet bags, a perfumed leather jerkin and other pleasant things. And that year the Queen had a pair of perfumed gloves trimmed only with four tufts or roses of coloured silk. The Queen took such pleasure in those gloves that she was pictured with those gloves upon her hands, and for many years after it was called the Earl of Oxford's perfume.' When the Earl left Court on one occasion (1578) it took eight carts to carry his stuff to London.

We have a portrait of him from 1575, very much the dandy, wearing a fashionable tall French hat of black velvet poised on one side of the head. The face, framed in a high ruff, is a perfect oval: almost hairless eyebrows, hardly at all a moustache, small voluptuous mouth and large sexy nose. It is a decidedly weak face.

The Protestant Duchess had noted of Lady Mary Vere that

their religions agreed not. And we learn later from the French
ambassador that, on Oxford's return from Italy, he had become
secretly a Catholic – thus justifying all that Burghley feared
from travel thither. This was in complete opposition to all that
he stood for, and no doubt Oxford's anti-Cecil complex entered
into it. Worse, he joined in association with the group of young
Catholic aristocrats who were in active opposition to the
régime and some of whom became exiles: Charles Arundel,
who was a member of George Gilbert's association for bringing
in seminary priests and supporting them,[2] Charles Paget and
his brother Lord Paget, Francis Southwell and inevitably, in the
background, Lord Henry Howard.

Oxford brought back with him not only Italian fashions but
Italianate tastes, if indeed he had not enjoyed them already –
they may well have been an element in his distaste for matrimony. A few years later when the group quarrelled and split
up, Oxford blew the gaff on it, returned to his duty to the
Queen and reported to her their misdoings. In return they were
willing enough, in self-defence, to split on him. Even when we
make allowance for exaggeration and for what was said *in
poculis* (in their cups), enough remains that is recognisably
Oxford's inflexion. His previous sympathy for Norfolk re-
appears in the charge that he had railed at him for giving up so
easily and 'not following his counsel at Lichfield to take arms'.
Oxford's friend Charles Arundel went on to depict him as 'a
shameless liar, an habitual drunkard', and to charge him with
blasphemy and 'buggering a boy that is his cook and many
other boys'.[3]

Under examination Arundel deposed, 'I will prove him a
buggerer of a boy that is his cook, by his own confession as well
as by witnesses. I have seen this boy many a time in his
chamber, doors close-locked, together with him, maybe at
Whitehall and at his house in Broad Street; and, finding it so, I
have gone to the backdoor to satisfy myself: at the which the
boy hath come out all in a sweat, and I have gone in and found
the beast in the same plight. But, to make it more apparent, my
Lord Harry saw more, and the boy confessed it unto Southwell,
and himself confirmed it unto Mr William Cornwallis.' Not to

go into further detail, we may add that Oxford had also an Italian page, 'Orache'. He had returned from Italy imbued with the view that 'Englishmen were dolts and nidwits' not to know that there was better sport than with women.

There was nothing surprising in this after all – it was just what Christopher Marlowe said, and these tastes were exemplified not only in this circle but by both Anthony and Francis Bacon. They also help to explain Oxford's breach with his wife.

The Earl continued his attendance at Court without any reconciliation with her, though she earnestly sought it. We find him engaged with other peers in presenting a masque to the Queen, or offering her costly jewels. We recognise his aristocratic haughtiness when the Queen asked him to dance at a ceremonial reception for the French ambassador: 'he replied that her Majesty would not order him to do so, as he did not wish to entertain Frenchmen. When the Lord Steward took him the message the second time, he replied that he would not give pleasure to Frenchmen nor listen to such a message. And with that he left the room.'

There followed the celebrated quarrel with Philip Sidney on the tennis-court – this would be the ancient game of real tennis – which has been so much written about. It seems trivial enough, except that it points to the difference of party-affiliation, Oxford in favour of the Anjou marriage (which makes his behaviour to the French ambassador the more inexcusable), Sidney, as a strong Protestant, vehemently opposed to it. Oxford was verging on thirty, Sidney four years younger; both were hot-tempered and tempers flared up over some trifle. The Earl called Sidney 'puppy', an insult for an Elizabethan, and repeated it. Sidney thereupon gave him the lie, and left the court. It seems very childish for grown men, but each sent the other a challenge. The Queen, whose business it was to keep order in the nursery, sent for Sidney and 'laid before him the difference in degree between earls and gentlemen, the respect inferiors owed to their superiors, the necessity in Princes to maintain their own creations . . . how the gentleman's neglect of the nobility taught the peasant to insult both'.

It gives us a fascinating glimpse of the rationale of class and degree, of the point of social deference, and the Queen's sense of her duty in maintaining the class structure. Sidney defended himself point by point and significantly appealed to Henry VIII's line, 'who gave the gentry free and safe appeal to his feet' against the oppression of the grandees. Indeed it was his policy to support the gentry against the nobility: an element in his widespread popularity. After this significant exchange, Sidney withdrew from Court for some time.

It was simply the fact that Oxford was an earl that made people overestimate such small contributions as he made to literature, along with the sense of deference to a grandee and the sycophancy from authors in need of patronage and reward. Earlier, for example, Oxford had written a Latin Preface to an English translation of Castiglione's *Courtier* – little enough in itself, yet Gabriel Harvey enthused, 'Let that courtly epistle, more polished even than the writings of Castiglione himself, witness how greatly thou dost excel in letters.'

As a poet Oxford was the best of a poor lot – the early Elizabethans – himself, like them (his uncle Golding, for example), much addicted to jogging fourteeners:

> Framed in the front of forlorn hope past all recovery
> I stayless stand, to abide the shock of shame and infamy.
> My life, through lingering long, is lodged in love of
>   loathsome ways;
> My death delayed to keep from life and harm of hapless
>   days.
> My sprites, my heart, my wit and force, in deep distress
>   are drowned;
> The only loss of my good name is of these griefs
>   the ground . . . .

The best that can be said for this is that it is a genuine poem, inspired, as Oxford usually was, by self-pity. It dates to the trouble of 1576, the scandal which he had needlessly created for himself. Fourteeners were popular with the earlier Elizabethans, as also the insensitive addiction to too much alliteration.

Even when the Earl's verse improved later, it is conventional enough, as in the best of his love-poems:

What cunning can express
The favour of her face,
To whom in this distress
I do appeal for grace?
A thousand Cupids fly
About her gentle eye:

From whence each throws a dart
That kindleth soft sweet fire
Within my sighing heart,
Possessèd by desire
No sweeter life I try
Than in her love to die . . .

This pleasant lily white,
This taint of roseate red,
This Cynthia's silver light,
This sweet fair Dea spread,
These sunbeams in mine eye:
These beauties make me die.

This is a song; to get a full idea of its effect, we must imagine it sung to the plangent cadences of the lute, in the glittering and bejewelled splendour of the Court. The references to the white rose and the red, and to Cynthia's silvery light, make it clear that it was addressed to the Virgin Queen, as was most of Ralegh's poetry contemporaneously.

Oxford's best-known lines are, however, addressed to himself:

Were I a king, I could command content;
Were I obscure, hidden should be my cares;
Or were I dead, no cares should me torment,
Nor hopes, nor hates, nor loves, nor griefs, nor fears.
A doubtful choice, of these three which to crave:
A kingdom, or a cottage, or a grave.

This has not ceased to move, and it brings us close to the spirit of the man who wrote it: for ever unsatisfied, discontented with himself, unhappy with his lot in life, well aware of the uncertainties that surround us, doubtful what choice of fortune were best.

Turn the page to his rival, Philip Sidney, and we at once notice the difference, the power, of a real poet, in just one line:

'Fool', said my Muse to me, 'look in thy heart and write.'

Or the reality of observation in such a line as

With how sad steps, O Moon, thou climb'st the skies!

Let alone compassion, the feeling for others of such sonnets as

Come, sleep, O sleep, the certain knot of peace,
   The baiting place of wit, the balm of woe,
The poor man's wealth, the prisoner's release,
   The indifferent judge between the high and low . . . .

So Italianate a figure as Oxford, bringing back the latest fashions thence, was an obvious target for satire, as in the appalling hexameters of Gabriel Harvey's 'Speculum Tuscanismi':

Since Galatea came in, and Tuscanism gan usurp,
Vanity above all . . . .
Delicate in speech, quaint in array: conceited in all points,
In Courtly guiles a passing singular odd man,
For gallants a brave mirror, a primrose of honour,
A diamond for nonce, a fellow peerless in England . . . .

That Oxford was aimed at – his characteristics recognisably hit off – is made clear from Harvey's tactless explanation: his 'noble lordship I protest I never meant to dishonour with the least prejudicial word of my tongue or pen. . . . The noble Earl, not disposed to trouble his Jovial [i.e. Jove-like] mind with such Saturnine poetry, still continued like his magnificent self.'

Oxford was ambivalent, like a good many other talented people – Southampton, for example. His interest in boys ready to hand did not exclude attentions to women, while still living apart from his wife. A Court-poem of the time, which may have been written by Oxford himself, alerts us to what was brewing: 'Anne Vavasour's Echo' portends to be a reply to the typical love-lorn suit of a male, in melancholy mood:

O heavens, who was the first that bred in me this fever? *Vere.*
Who was the first that gave the wound whose fear I wear
 for ever? *Vere.*
What tyrant, Cupid, to my harm usurps thy golden
 quiver? *Vere.*
What wight first caught this hart, and can from bondage
 it deliver? *Vere.*

The verses are apposite enough to the situation: someone knew well enough what was afoot, or in hand.

In March 1581 the sober Walsingham reports, 'on Tuesday at night Anne Vavasour was brought to bed of a son in the maidens' chamber'. This was a scandal very close to the Queen, of a kind that infuriated that spinsterly deity. 'The Earl of Oxford is avowed to be the father, who hath withdrawn himself with intent, as it is thought, to pass the seas. The ports are laid for him and therefore, if he have any such determination, it is not likely that he will escape. The gentlewoman, the selfsame night she was delivered, was conveyed out of the house and committed to the Tower. Others that have been found any ways party to the cause have also been committed. Her Majesty is greatly grieved with the accident.'

Oxford also was committed to the Tower. Once more he was in serious trouble, once more the burden fell upon Burghley to get him out of it. In June Oxford was released; shortly before he wrote to acknowledge 'how honourably you had dealt with her Majesty as touching my liberty, as this day she had made promises to your lordship that it shall be. Unless your lordship shall make some motion to put her Majesty in mind

thereof, I fear she will forget me.' Then, loftily as ever, he
makes the reproach, 'for she is nothing of her own disposition,
as I find, so ready to deliver as speedy to commit, and every
little trifle gives her matter for a long delay'. The Queen would
not grant him full liberty until he had taken back his wife.

Even so, upon his release from the Tower the Earl refused to
conform to the usual custom of yielding his upper garment as a
perquisite to the Lieutenant – on the ground that 'he may not a
little be touched in honour if he shall be brought to yield unto a
custom only upon persons committed to that place for treason'.
There we have him, always standing on his dignity, making a
fuss about his 'honour'. The trivial matter came before the
Privy Council, and as usual he got his way.

'Every little trifle'! – as if the sovereign lady had not a
hundred more important matters on her mind in 1581, with the
critical turn of affairs in Scotland, the complex crisis in the
Netherlands, the intricate difficulties over the Anjou marriage,
the gathering conflict with Spain. These matters took up
Burghley's mind and time equally. Elizabeth's resentment
was marked; she kept Oxford away from Court for the next
two years.

Nor was the Vavasour affair without its further trail of
troubles during these years. Though Burghley called the young
woman, crisply, a 'drab', her family and friends resented the
irreparable damage to her reputation: she was no longer mar-
riageable. In March 1582 Oxford was challenged by one of her
relations; there followed 'a fray between my Lord of Oxford
and Mr Thomas Knyvet of the Privy Chamber, who were both
hurt, but my Lord of Oxford more dangerously. Mr Knyvet is
not meanly beloved in Court, and therefore he is not like to
speed ill, whatsoever the quarrel be.' That means that Oxford
was blamed and Knyvet not likely to be charged. Oxford recovered, but the followers of the two men carried on the feud in
the Elizabethan manner. In June two of the Earl's men were
wounded in a fray with Knyvet's men in Lambeth Marsh. Then
an attack upon Knyvet himself was instigated as he was making
for Blackfriars Stairs upon the river. In July Knyvet killed one

of his assailants in an affray. Next spring one of Oxford's men killed Knyvet's Long Tom. Even two years later Thomas Vavasour challenged the Earl: 'if thy body had been as deformed as thy mind is dishonourable, my house had as yet been unspotted, and thyself remained with thy cowardice unknown . . . Use not thy birth for an excuse, for I am a gentleman, but meet me thyself alone, and thy lackey to hold thy horse.'

The repeated use of the term 'thy' to a social superior was in itself an insult to Elizabethans. We see how true to the life of the time *Romeo and Juliet* is, for all its fashionable Italian colouring. The Queen was disturbed by the continuing affair, and Burghley had further cause for grief. He did his best to defend Oxford, as always, trying to enlist the favourite Hatton's support to allay the Queen's anger, 'perceiving by my Lord of Leicester some increase of her Majesty's offence towards my Lord of Oxford'. All Burghley could say was that 'I submit all these things to God's will, who knoweth best why it pleaseth him to afflict my Lord of Oxford in this sort, who hath, I confess, forgotten his duty to God.' Then, with a sigh, 'and yet I hope he may be made a good servant to her Majesty, if it please her of her clemency to remit her displeasure for his fall in her Court – which is not twice-yeared, and he punished as far or farther than any like crime hath been: first by her Majesty, and then by the drab's friend in revenge to the peril of his life'.

No marriage for her now, the drab took refuge in the arms of Sir Henry Lee. Not yet was Oxford's offence forgiven, or himself permitted to return to Court. In the midst of his trials his wife, good woman, made yet another effort to get him to return to her arms – after five years. In December 1582 she wrote, 'my Lord, in what misery I may account myself to be that neither can see any end thereof nor yet any hope to diminish it. And now of late having had some hope that your lordship would have renewed some part of your favour that you began to show me this summer, though you seemed fearful how to show it by open address.' That means, pride forbade him to acknowledge how deeply he had wronged her. She did not say that, merely affirmed, as she had all along, that his 'misliking of me [was] without any cause in deed or thought'. She appealed to him not 'to be led still to detain me in calamity without some probable cause, whereof, I appeal to God, I am utterly innocent'.

All the world knew that she was. Now, in the midst of the troubles he had brought on his own head, he was ready for a reconciliation, at least privately, and to accept her into his own house to live together again. This was at least a step towards his eventual return to Court. It was, however, delayed. Another of Burghley's daughters was dying, and he himself was ill and depressed. He and his wife had made long intercession with the Queen, but so far without avail. 'But hereof I will in no wise complain of too much hardness but to myself.' Then, with unwonted but understandable bitterness: 'both I and she are determined to suffer and lament our misfortune that, when our son-in-law was in prosperity, he was a cause of our adversity by his unkind usage of us and ours. And now that he is ruined and in adversity, we only are made partakers thereof and by no means, no, not by the bitter tears of my wife, can obtain a spark of favour for him.'

A recognised way to please the Queen, or to celebrate return to favour, was to present entertainments for her solace and recreation at Court or on progress through the country. In 1579 Oxford had taken part in a Shrovetide device at Court, and on another occasion he presented a masque with Lord Windsor and other peers. His intellectual interests were mainly literary, in extending patronage to needy authors whose books he apparently 'perused', and to a lesser extent in drama; sometimes these interests coincided. In 1579 Anthony Munday had dedicated *The Mirror of Mutability* to him; Munday was taken into the Earl's service, for next year he dedicated to him *Zelanto, the Fountain of Fame* as his 'servant': 'my simple self (Right Honourable) having sufficiently seen the rare virtues of your noble mind, the heroical qualities of your prudent person . . .'. After that exordium we may better judge the qualities attributed to Oxford by writers hoping for gratification: in some measure tributes like this to a noble peer were in accordance with the

Elizabethan sense of decorum – like Shakespeare's flowery language to his patron – but we are reminded not 'to confuse social deference with literary criticism'.

At the end of 1578 John Lyly had published his *Euphues: The Anatomy of Wit*, which had prodigious influence at the time. Lyly had been Burghley's scholar at Magdalen College, Oxford, supported at least in part by the great man. At this time he had lodgings in the Savoy, which was under Burghley's authority; the proximity is enough to account for Oxford's taking Lyly also under his wing. In 1582 he dedicated the sequel, *Euphues and his England*, to Oxford in the usual obsequious terms: 'I know none more fit to defend it than one of the Nobility of England, nor any of the Nobility more ancient or more honourable than your lordship. . . . I could not find one more noble in Court than your honour, who is or should be under her Majesty chiefest in Court, by birth born to the greatest office, and therefore methought by right to be placed in great authority. For whoso compareth the honour of your lordship's noble house with the fidelity of your ancestors may well say, which no other can truly gainsay, *Vero nihil verius* [nothing more true than the true man].'

The last sentence is true enough and Oxford's precursor the 13th Earl – to whose fidelity the Tudor dynasty owed so much – had had his troupe of players back in Henry VII's reign. In 1580 two of our Earl's servants were committed to Marshalsea for a fray with some young lawyers: one of the servants was a well-known actor, Laurence Dutton. Oxford not only had men among the players who wore his badge, but – we are not surprised to learn – also boys: there is a trace of 'the Earl of Oxford's lads' playing at Norwich in 1580–1, and at Bristol in September 1581 we learn that they were nine boys under the conduct of one man.

After Oxford's return to Court a troupe of his servants performed there on New Year's day and 3 March 1584: their payee was Lyly, still apparently in the Earl's service. At Christmas this year a performance of *Agamemnon and Ulysses* was given by his boys, 'on St John's day at night at Greenwich', when the payee was Henry Evans. Presumably Lyly left his service and the boys' troupe came to an end, for at New Year 1585 the Earl's men servants performed feats of vaulting and acrobatics at Court. His players did not appear again at Court, so we must conclude that they were not in any way important or good; they can be traced in the provinces. Much later, in 1602, what was left of his troupe merged with the Earl of Worcester's men, who in turn became Queen Anne's men.

And that is all there is to it. When we hear of noblemen like Ferdinando, Lord Strange, 'penning comedies', of which nothing remains, or of Lord Oxford as 'deserving the highest prize for comedy and interlude', these phrases are not to be taken to amount to much – perhaps no more than that these peers took a personal interest in the work of their comedians. Lyly worked with other combinations of boy players, the children of the royal Chapel and St Paul's boys, training and producing them, along with Oxford's, in Blackfriars. There their premises were taken over by Lord Chamberlain Hunsdon in 1585.

From what Thomas Watson says, in his dedication of his *Hekatompathia, the Passionate Century of Love*, it appears that Oxford took a personal interest in the work of his authors: 'the world hath understood (I know not how) that your honour had willingly vouchsafed the acceptance of this work, and at convenient leisures favourably perused it, being as yet but in written hand'. Watson became the close friend of Christopher Marlowe, whose work had hardly yet appeared on the stage. His senior, and acquaintance, Robert Greene had, who dedicated in 1584 *Greene's Card of Fancy* thus: 'wheresoever Maecenas lodgeth, thither no doubt will scholars flock. And your honour being a worthy favourer and fosterer of learning hath forced many through your excellent virtue to offer the first-fruits of their study at the shrine of your lordship's courtesy.'

We need hardly go further into the tale of dedications: we know that the Earl was extravagant, and no doubt he was generous. When John Farmer came to dedicate his first songbook to him, we find again this note of exaggeration: 'those that know your lordship have overgone most of them that make it a profession'. Now we know how to interpret these tributes.

When we hear of 'The Earl of Oxford's March', or 'The Earl of Oxford's Galliard', it does not mean that they are his compositions, but that they were given his name by their composers. Oxford had more extravagant, and less remunerative, ways of wasting his substance. In these middle years we find him sinking a huge sum of money in Frobisher's nugatory voyages in pursuit of auriferous ore on the coast of Labrador. Oxford invested £3000 in the second of these voyages, which brought back no gold-bearing ore: all were losers, Oxford worst of all, since, gambler that he was, his was the biggest investment. Not content with this loss, he made another with Fenton's abortive voyage of 1582 – this time of £500. (Multiply for contemporary valuation!) He was selling land right and left, until hardly anything was left of his splendid inheritance. Meanwhile Burghley was building up a second inheritance in the south, for his clever younger son, and building a second palace, in addition to Burghley, namely Theobalds, for Robert Cecil one day to succeed to. That must have been galling for the Earl of ancient family. In all he made fifty-six separate sales of land, of which nearly half were effected during these unhappy middle years, 1577 to 1581. What a great fool he was!

The return to his wife eased his return to Court and the favour of the respectable Queen. It was, interestingly enough, the new favourite, Ralegh, who effected it. Rutland was told, 'Master Ralegh was a great mean [i.e. means], whereat Pondus is angry for that he could not do so much.' Pondus was, no doubt, Burghley, who had received a 'discomfortable answer' to his representations. So Ralegh explained himself to the great man, 'that her Majesty would never permit anything to be prosecuted to the Earl's danger – if any possibility were – and that therefore it were to small purpose, after so long absence and so many disgraces, to call his honour again in question, whereby he might appear the less fit either for her presence or favour. Her Majesty confessed that she meant it [further disfavour] only thereby to give the Earl warning.'
Ralegh had presented Burghley's appeal to the Queen,

reminding her 'how honourable and profitable it were for her Majesty to have regard to your lordship's health and quiet'. Elizabeth responded with a simply regal letter of comfort, the kind of thing that won her servants' hearts in spite of everything:

> Sir Spirit. I doubt I do misname you. For those of your kind (they say) have no sense. But I have of late seen an *ecce signum* [behold the sign] that if an ass kick you, you feel it too soon. I will recant you from being my *Spirit*, if ever I perceive that you disdain not such a feeling. Serve God, fear the king, and be a good fellow to the rest. Let never care appear in you for such a rumour. . . . And pass of no man so much as not to regard her trust, who putteth it in you.
>
> God bless you, and long may you last, *Omnino* [in everything], E. R.

Ralegh realised the danger he incurred by his intervention, but assured Burghley that 'I am content, for your sake, to lay the serpent before the fire as much as in me lieth – that, having recovered strength, myself may be most in danger of his poison and sting.' Oxford expressed no gratitude to the favourite, otherwise so far below him in rank: he called him loftily 'the Knave'. We see well how the Earl, for all his rank, was regarded; the Queen relented and 'after some bitter words and speeches, in the end all sins are forgiven and he may repair to Court at his leisure'.

The acute sense he had of his caste comes out in his plea for his fellow aristocrat Lord Lumley, in disgrace for his part in Norfolk's conspiracies. Oxford wrote on behalf of his kinsman, 'among all the rest of my blood this only remains in account either of me or else of them – the rest having embraced further alliances to leave their nearer consanguinity. And as I hope your lordship doth account me now – on whom you have so much bound – as I am: so be you before any else in the world, both through match – whereby I count my greatest stay – and by your lordship's friendly usage and sticking by me in this time wherein I am hedged in with so many enemies.'

We may be sure that Burghley knew his mood would not last. When he summoned Lyly to his presence, Oxford thought it 'very strange that your lordship should enter into that course towards me: whereby I must learn that which I knew not before, both of your opinion and good will towards me. But I pray, my lord, leave that course, for I mean not to be your ward nor your child. I serve her Majesty, and I am that I am [i.e. the premier Earl]; and scorn to be offered that injury to think I am so weak of government as to be ruled by servants, or not able to govern myself.'

But this was exactly what he was – and here we see the complex revealed going back to his early days. Back he was once more, a gilded ornament at Court – nothing more – taking part in a tilt at the end of 1584. Graver things were at hand: in 1585 the government had to intervene openly in the Netherlands or they would have been subjugated by Spain. It was decided to send an army there under Leicester. Oxford wanted employment. To Burghley, inevitably, he resorted: 'being now almost at a point to taste that good which her Majesty shall determine, yet I am as one that hath long besieged a fort and not able to compass the end or reap the fruit of his travail, being forced to levy his siege for want of munition'. Would Burghley lend him £200 until her Majesty came up with something?

He may have done, for at the end of August Oxford crossed over to Flushing, where Sir Philip Sidney was in command. By October the Earl was back in England, Secretary Davison reported, 'upon what humour I know not'. It was pretty clear that nobody wanted him, and that he was good for nothing.

Next year came a surprising move, which has mystified people who know little of the ways of the Elizabethan Court. Oxford was awarded a large pension of £1000 a year. How to explain it? For what services, they wonder. For none. It was simply the fact that here was the premier Earl, Lord Great Chamberlain of England, without visible means of support and quite unqualified, as everything shows, to occupy a responsible post. The Queen and her Lord Treasurer must have agreed upon this move, to stop his importunity and give him something to live upon. Meanwhile, it fell to Burghley to support all three of Oxford's daughters.

In spite of this he continued to level reproaches at his father-in-law, railing at his wife against her father, so as 'she spent all the evening in dolour and weeping. Though I did as much as I could comfort her with hope,' wrote Burghley, 'yet she, being as she is great with child, and continually afflicted to behold the misery of her husband and of his children, to whom he will not leave a farthing of land.' Their grandfather would have to look after them and provide most of their dowries – as he eventually did. 'Neither honour nor land nor goods shall come to their children; for whom, being three already to be kept and a fourth like to follow, I only am at charge even with sundry families in sundry places for their sustenance. But, if their father was of that good nature as to be thankful for the same, I would be less grieved with the burden.' No wonder he concluded with what he often had cause to think: 'No enemy I have can envy me this match.'

Oxford's line of conduct remained what it always had been: in his own words, 'always I have and I will still prefer mine own content before others'. As for the poor lady his wife – much loved by Burghley – she was shortly beyond her troubles: in June 1588 she died, still only thirty-two. She was buried in the Abbey with all appropriate pomp and a grand monument raised above her. Her father took the children into his house and care.

It was Armada time, and everybody – except for Oxford's friend the Earl of Arundel, who had masses said for its success – was keyed up to serve. Oxford was given a command in his own area at Harwich. Leicester, who was in supreme command, said that it was a post of honour, 'a place of great trust and great danger', as it would be if the Armada should round the coast there. Two thousand men were to be under Oxford's command. 'My Lord seemed at the first to like well of it', and the Queen gave 'her gracious consent of his willingness to serve her'. Then came a characteristic about-turn: Oxford came to Leicester and 'told me he thought the place of no service nor credit; and therefore he would to the Court and understand her Majesty's further pleasure'. At that moment, with the Armada in the Channel, Leicester instructed Walsingham, 'I must desire you – as I know her Majesty will also make him know – that it was good grace to appoint that place to him, having no more experience than he hath.' Oxford was now a man approaching forty. Leicester: 'for my own part being gladder to be rid of him than to have him, but only to have him contented'.

That was what they all thought – except that there was no contenting him. He was really fit only for ceremonial occasions; and when the Queen rode in state that November to give thanks at St Paul's for the victory over the Armada, he followed immediately on her right as Lord Great Chamberlain. So they processed up the long nave of old St Paul's, the Queen under a golden canopy borne by her grandees.

In 1591 Oxford married again, a young lady in waiting to the Queen, Elizabeth Trentham, daughter of a respectable knight and, it would seem, a pretty girl. The marriage turned out happily enough: this time the Earl chose for himself, instead of being caught by the girl. He had that about him with which to content a woman if he chose. Early in 1593 his young wife gave birth to a son and heir, who succeeded as 18th Earl. Burghley had to provide for Anne's daughters. He intended the eldest, Elizabeth, for another of his wards, the young Southampton, who had given a promise that he would marry her.[4] This he would not, and did not do, when he came of age to marry – in 1591 he was eighteen. Everybody was distressed by his reluctance, and then refusal – for which, in the event, he paid handsomely, for it amounted to breach of promise. His mother was rendered anxious, so was her father, Lord Montagu, who remonstrated with his grandson – whose poet was brought into the contest, to write the Sonnets to incline his youthful patron to the idea of marriage. Here was another spoiled young aristocrat who took against his guardian, the great Lord Treasurer.

However, Burghley was able to find a grander husband for Elizabeth in the Earl of Derby. Another of the granddaughters, Bridget, married Lord Norris of Rycote; an invalidish lady, she became a client of 'Dr' Forman, so that we at least know her complaints. The third was married to the handsome Philip Herbert, who became Earl of Montgomery.

In spite of the large pension he was receiving to keep him quiet, Oxford continued to pester his father-in-law and the

Queen for a job. He had already badgered them for the Presidency of Wales. No notice was taken – imagine what would happen under his Presidency! Now in 1593 he wanted the stewardship of the Forest of Essex, presumably Epping Forest with much larger circuit then – and received a piece of her mind from the Queen: 'I found that so displeasing unto her that, in place of receiving that ordinary favour which is of course granted to the meanest subject, I was brow-beaten and had many bitter speeches given me.'

When Burghley died in 1598, leaving considerable bequests of money, plate and goods to Oxford's daughters, the incorrigible Earl transferred his suits and badgering requests to his brother-in-law, Sir Robert Cecil. Might he have the governorship of Jersey? It was awarded to Sir Walter Ralegh. When Essex was executed, after his rebellion, the news was brought to the Queen as she was playing on the virginals, Ralegh in attendance. Oxford, who was not without wit, commented, 'when Jacks start up, heads go down' – a demeaning reference to Ralegh, who actually came from an ancient, but impoverished, family.

Oxford had impoverished himself. His later correspondence is filled with requests for money or gambler-like projects for making it. At one time he suggests that his annuity of £1000 might be commuted for a downright sum of £5000 – this would have been fatal, spent in no time. The pension, regularly paid as it was – not everyone was so fortunate – at least enabled him to live modestly at his wife's place in Hackney. We spare the reader the long and involved letters in which he spun hopeful projects for making money with the merchant Carmarden. At another time he enters into negotiation with the foremost tin-merchants in Cornwall, the Roberts family in Truro – to become the Lords Robartes in the next generation – to purchase the pre-emption of tin, i.e. the monopoly of its sale. The Earl puts forward the usual gambler's calculations as to how profitable it would be for everybody. We need not burden the reader with his financial fantasies.

However, the thought suggests something to the mind: he would appear to have been a *fantaisiste*. Once more – might he become President of Wales?

On Elizabeth's death he wrote a charming letter to his brother-in-law, Cecil. He had been bidden to the reception of the new king at Whitehall early in the morning: 'which being impossible, yet I hasted so much as I came to follow you into Ludgate, though – through press of people and horses – I could not reach your company as I desired, but followed as I might'. And then, recalling the past: 'I cannot but find great grief in myself to remember the Mistress which we have lost, under whom both you and myself from our greenest years have been, in a manner, brought up. . . . We cannot look for so much left of our days as to bestow upon another neither the long acquaintance and kind familiarities wherewith she did use us.'

Elizabeth had done her best for him and well requited the debt which her dynasty owed to the 13th Earl. But she had failed with the 17th, failed in precisely what she set herself to do with the young men she favoured at her Court – to turn them into good servants of the state – and this through the all too obvious defects of character of the young Earl who had begun with promise, with some gifts of mind and a good education. He had accomplished nothing with his life, and left only a few poems, good for their date and kind.

At James I's coronation Oxford made his last public appearance: as Lord Great Chamberlain it fell to him to dress the King, and to serve him with ewer and basin to wash his hands at the feast in Westminster Hall. Presumably in requital, he at last obtained the stewardship of Essex Forest and the keepership of the royal house and park at Havering. This was his last year.

The house to which he had retired, the 'King's Place' in Hackney, had been bought by his second wife. We have indications that in his last years he was something of an invalid, and he was only fifty-four when he died on 24 June 1604. It was his widow who provided that a plain monument should be set up for them both, 'fitting our degree'.

This is all, and indeed rather more than all, that we wish to know of the 17th Earl of Oxford.

SOURCES *Calendars of State Papers Domestic*; *Historical MSS Commission, Hastings* and *Rutland MSS*; G. E. C. (ed.), *Cock-*

ayne's *Peerage*; E. K. Chambers, *The Elizabethan Stage*, II;
B. M. Ward, *The Seventeenth Earl of Oxford*, cites many docu-
ments, but the judgments are not to be relied on; Conyers Read,
Lord Burghley and Queen Elizabeth; G. K. Hunter, *John Lyly*;
E. K. Chambers, *Sir Henry Lee*; L. T. Golding, *An Elizabethan
Puritan: The Life of Arthur Golding* – the title however is mis-
taken: Golding, though a Protestant, was not a Puritan.

4

Elizabeth I's Godson: Sir John Harington

I

IR John Harington is an underestimated writer. There are various reasons for this. He has come down to us as Queen Elizabeth's 'witty godson', as she described him; but we must remember that with Elizabethans 'witty' had a more extended sense: it meant, generally, clever and intelligent. Then too, he spread himself rather widely: a writer of epigrams both 'pleasant and serious'; a translator not only of Ariosto's *Orlando Furioso* but of a medical treatise of the School of Salerno, *The Englishman's Doctor*. Even the book that made him notorious as Sir 'Ajax' Harington, *The Metamorphosis of Ajax* [A Jakes]: *A New Discourse of a Stale Subject*, a comic treatise on privies putting forward his invention of the water-closet, has its serious side, for he was interested in health and sanitation. He wrote a number of tracts, always from a sensible point of view, on Ireland, on the succession to the throne, on play, besides an informative account of the bishops of the Church of England.

Mandell Creighton, in his account of him in the *Dictionary of National Biography*, describes him as 'miscellaneous writer' – which he was; but the phrase has a somewhat derogatory connotation, when Harington was a considerable writer, well worthy of consideration. Lytton Strachey hardly considered him, in an essay which is not much more than a squib. Creighton, who was a real historian, did better: Harington, he says, 'gives a living picture of life and society in his times, and abounds in incidental stories which throw great light upon many prominent persons'. He suggests that a detailed biography 'would present an interesting sketch of Elizabethan times'; yet no one has had the sense to write one, when we are presented instead with scores of biographies of Elizabeth or Mary Queen of Scots. As a poet, too, Creighton says, 'he has received scanty justice from posterity'. Harington regarded himself quite rightly as no mere versifier – as it might be a Thomas Churchyard, an Arthur Brooke or even a Gascoigne. Though he did not reach any height of eloquence or inspiration, he was a natural poet to whom numbers came easily, with always a point to make. Then Creighton falls down through Victorian prudery: Harington 'resembles Sterne at his worst no less in his curious and varied learning than in his indecency'.

So far from that being a discommendation, it recommends both to us in our time: they present us with the whole of life as it is, not a castrated view of it. Actually both Harington and Sterne are more subtle: they get their effects by innuendo, rather than by crude bawdry. They are suggestive writers, in both senses of the word, and all the more interesting. As Harington says, we live among men and not among saints – let alone the plaster saints of the Victorian age and of conventional humbug. He was very human, as well as a humanist – and even Sir Thomas More enjoyed scatological jokes, in the indecent obscurity of Latin.

Harington prided himself on his familiar letters. He would have agreed with the great scholar Selden that 'the complexion of the times and manners of men are best seen in familiar letters on private matters; for when men write to the multitude they cloak their own thoughts in the hopes or fears of others'. Harington is natural and unconstrained, and all the better reading. Thus he is an endearing, if not an enchanting, figure. He comes through to us as a natural human being, crystal-clear, not clogged by pretence or pretension. He has the naïveté of a clever man, who is not afraid of appearing clever to tone himself down to the level of the conventional and dull, or to fall into the clichés of the merely sophisticated afraid to give themselves away. Harington gives himself away on every page: that is why he is alive, where they are dead.

He was much more besides this: not only an observer of men's ways, but a connoisseur of art and architecture, and a collector. He collected to some point – a remarkable library of the stage plays of his time, the complete catalogue of which remains, a valuable index for historians of the Elizabethan theatre.

Harington had an exceptional background which brought him close to Elizabeth I, made him her godson and an intimate of hers; hence he enjoyed a privileged view of her and her Court. His father came from ancient Cumbrian stock which suffered losses in the Wars of the Roses; then the family came to centre upon Exton in Rutland, where one sees the tombs of the senior branch. How John's father, the elder John Harington, came to Somerset is a curious tale. Treasurer of the King's camps and buildings, he married a natural daughter of Henry VIII, who had been brought up by the royal tailor as his own. She brought with her a goodly dowry of some of the pleasant lands of Bath Abbey at Kelston and Batheaston in Somerset. She died leaving him her property, and he recommended himself to the service of Princess Elizabeth. Among her ladies-in-waiting he found his second wife, Isabella Markham, to whom he wrote charming poems, for he was one of the better poets of the time. During Wyatt's rebellion against Queen Mary, the couple were sent to the Tower along with the Princess Elizabeth, 'only for carrying a letter', the son said. The elder Harington remained faithful to Elizabeth through her early vicissitudes, and received his reward. As Queen she seems to have been fond of her gifted godson and allowed him more liberties than most. He returned her affection, along with a proper awe; we owe to him private glimpses of her in her last years which are both revealing and moving.

Born in 1561 the young Harington was evidently well educated at Eton, whither the Queen expedited a copy of her speech to the Parliament of 1575 with the typically sentential adjuration to 'ponder these poor words in thy hours of leisure, and play with them till they enter thine understanding'. He went on to King's College, Cambridge, for a couple of years, 1576–8, where he received the benefit of tuition from the excellent John Still and advice from the great Lord Burghley. It was good of the Queen's Lord Treasurer, amid all the burdens and chores of his office, to write to the lad at length, giving him detailed advice about his studies and conduct. 'I thank you, my good Jack, for your letters which I like, not for the praise they give me but for the promise they make me: that is, that you will continue your endeavour to get understanding, without which a man is little accounted of, and indeed cannot tell truly how to account of himself.' After taking the trouble to lay down a course of reading and study, the great man concluded, 'so you shall become a comfort to your father and praise to your master, an honour to the university, a fit servant for the Queen and your country for which you were born . . . which I that loves you both wish and hope of. And so commend me to you, my good Jack, and us both to God's goodness, Your father's friend that loves you.' The letter does credit to both, but chiefly to the wise old man who administered the country with such discretion.

At Cambridge the youth was beholden to John Still, who later became his diocesan as Bishop of Bath and Wells, to whom Harington paid a sincere tribute: 'to whom I never came but I grew more religious, from whom I never went but I parted better instructed'. The pupil proved a credit to his master: he was a faithful and helpful servant of the Church of England, who took a foremost part in re-roofing semi-ruined Bath Abbey, and he was certainly well instructed in languages and literature, ancient and modern. He was also, like the bishop, no precise Puritan but loved music: Dr Still could 'sing well, in which last he hath good judgment, and I have heard good music of voices in his house'. Among many tit-bits of information about Court life, he tells us that Henry VIII when in a good mood would sing a verse against the monks which Harington's father had composed, the 'Black Sanctus', the music too, for he had been trained up in music by Tallis. (Henry, who loved music, took Tallis from service with the monks at Waltham Abbey into the Chapel Royal.) Young Harington, who kept everything, preserved the music of this song, copied out by his amanuensis, Thomas Combe.

Stage plays, especially in Latin, performed a useful part in education at school and at the university. Harington coincided at one play with another in whose education Burghley took an interest, the young Earl of Essex, then at Trinity. Harington, the reverse of a sourpuss, defends plays: 'I remember in Cambridge, howsoever the preciser sort have banished them, the wiser sort did – and still do – maintain them.' He thought that tragedy especially had a good moral effect and recalled the famous Latin play on Richard III, by Thomas Legge, acted at St John's in 1579. 'Then for comedies, how full of harmless mirth is our Cambridge *Pedantius*?' – this was a skit on the pedant Gabriel Harvey – 'and the Oxford *Bellum Grammaticale*?' This was performed before the Queen on her visit in 1592, with the two Cambridge men, Essex and Southampton, with probably William Shakespeare in attendance on the latter. It would seem too that Harington was present and saw the play. He then goes on to commend a London play called *The Play of Cards*.

The Queen continued to take an interest in her godson's education, for in this year 1579 she gave him a piece of her own translation from Cicero and later another out of Seneca. The inner Court circle was highly educated, worthy to compare with a Renaissance Court in Italy – and Creighton compares Harington's later role with that of a Court wit at one of them.

After Cambridge, Lincoln's Inn, in the regular manner for a young gentleman; marriage and building his house for his family at Kelston. In the 1580s he married Mary, daughter of Sir George Rogers of Cannington, a proper county alliance; they lived happily together, no marital troubles to incur the Queen's disapprobation. We have a double portrait of the couple: Mary a rather homely body, no beauty but with a pleasantly humorous upturned mouth. John was a handsome man, oval head, dark hair and well-arched eyebrows; fine, intelligent, wide-apart eyes; everything sharp and pointed, pointed beard and moustaches, a very wide-awake expression.

Many of Harington's epigrams were addressed to his wife and were love poems, for they were happily matched. One of them is 'to comfort her for the loss of her children' – two had died, a small proportion for an Elizabethan family.

> When at thy window thou thy doves are feeding,
> Then think I shortly my Dove will be breeding,
> Like will love like, and so my liking like thee,
> As I to doves in many things can like thee . . .
> Both murmur kindly, both are often billing,
> Yet both to Venus' sports will seem unwilling . . .

He goes further on this theme, into his own male lust:

> Thou tell'st me, Mall, and I believe it must,
> That thou canst love me much with little lust;
> But while of this chaste love thou dost devise
> And look'st chaste babies in my wanton eyes,
> Thy want of lust makes my lust wanton-wise . . .
> I cannot love thee long without my lust.

Sex with his wife did not lose its appeal for him; when she wanted something from him, 'a velvet gown or some rich border', she appealed to him with

> Thy locks, thy lips, thy looks speak all in order,
> Thou think'st – and right thou think'st – that these
>   do move me . . .
> But shall I tell thee what most thy suit advances?
> Thy fair smooth words? No, no: thy fair smooth
>   haunches.

After fourteen years of married life he could write,

> Two prenticeships with thee I now have been,
> Mad times, sad times, glad times, our life hath seen:
> Souls we have wrought four pair since our first meeting
> Of which two souls, sweet souls, were to be fleeting.

My workmanship so well doth please thee still,
Thou wouldst not grant me freedom by thy will;[1]
And I'll confess such usage have I found,
Mine heart yet ne'er desired to be unbound . . . .

He was several years in building the family home at Kelston,
a fine mansion of which nothing, alas, now remains: rebuilt in
the eighteenth century. Nor are there any memorials of him in
the church: his writings are his memorial. He wrote to Burghley that he was 'busy with my workmen, yet idle myself, I
write naught but long bills. Well in my body, but sick in my
purse. Merry to think my house is well nigh done, and sad to
say 'tis not well nigh paid for.' That was a good hint, but he got
nothing out of the Lord Treasurer or the Queen, except their
good will and personal favour; and he was extravagant. We
have the orders that he indicted for his household, with characteristic touches. 'That no servant be absent from prayer at
morning or evening. . . . That no man make water within either
of the courts, upon pain of – every time it shall be proved –
1*d*. . . . That none toy with the maids, on pain of 4*d*.'

Meanwhile he was writing and circulating the epigrams
which brought him his reputation as a Court wit – and give
such insights into the life of the time, much to its taste – but
were not published until after his death. For the ladies at Court
he translated one of the more suggestive stories from Ariosto's
Orlando Furioso. The Queen, who was no prude, pretended that
he was corrupting the morals of her ladies and suggested that he
stay at home until he had translated the whole work. It was
published in 1591, printed by Richard Field in Blackfriars, who
printed Shakespeare's poems two and three years later. (There
was much in sympathy between those two minds.) A whole
literature of translation grew up, from many languages – part of
the education of the up-and-coming country. Harington's
Ariosto made its own mark, for the romantic poem of medieval
chivalry was in keeping with the tone of the age, or its idea of
itself.

His Preface, 'A Brief Apology for Poetry', also makes a mark
of its own. It has been regarded too simply as a sequel to Philip

Sidney's more celebrated *Defence*, but Harington's own individuality comes through. In that age everybody was writing verse, 'being a thing that everybody that never scarce baited their horse at the university take upon them to make'. However, 'some grave men misliked that I should spend so much good time on such a trifling work as they deemed a Poem to be'. (Was Burghley one of these?) There always will be such men – boring Poloniuses: one wonders why Harington thought it necessary to excuse himself to such people, unless he had Burghley in mind, or to defend poetry at all.

Poetry, he says rightly, is 'the very first nurse and ancient grandmother of all learning'. Translators had been depreciated as mere versifiers: he asked pertinently whether this held for Lucan (translated by Marlowe, though he doesn't mention him), Phaer's Virgil, or Golding's Ovid? He replies roundly that writing verse is 'a gift, not an art'. We may regard it as both, but certainly he had the gift: writing verse came easily to him, perhaps he would have achieved more lasting fame if he had worked at it more as an art – after all, he was a gentleman amateur, not a professional. He had a natural gift for rhythm and rhyme (unlike many modern 'poets') and the true poet's instinct: 'the words being couched together in due order, measure and number, one doth as it were bring on another, as myself have often proved'. And, 'I have ever found that verse is easier to learn and far better to preserve in memory than is prose.' It is a prime disadvantage of verse without rhyme or scansion today that it is unmemorable.

For Harington's easy, ambling versification we may cite Rogero's journey to the rescue of Angelica, often represented in Renaissance painting:

> Wherefore to make the people marvel more
>   And, as it were, to sport himself and play,
> He spurred his beast, who straight aloft did soar,
>   And bare his master westward quite away;
> And straight he was beyond our English shore,
>   Meaning to pass the Irish seas that day;
>   St George's Channel in a little while
>   He passed, and after saw the Irish isle.

Where men do tell strange tales that long ago
St Patrick built a solitary cave,
Into the which they that devoutly go
By purging of their sins their souls may save;
Now whether this report be true or no
I not affirm, and yet I not deprave,
Crossing from hence to islandward he found
Angelica unto the rock fast bound.

Naked and bound at this same Isle of Woe,
For Isle of Woe it may be justly called . . . .

He was to find that to be true shortly, from his own experience.
The suggestive side to his mind was always alive, ready to give
(or take) a hint:

But viewing nearer he was quickly taught,
She had some parts that were not made of plaster . . .
This said, she blushed, seeing those parts were spied
The which, though fair, yet nature strives to hide.

Harington's work has been criticised as a 'paraphrase' rather
than a translation; but he was quite right to abbreviate and omit
digressions, rather than to translate literally – and be unread-
able. As it is, his is very readable, more so than many
Elizabethan translations: he added a work, in its own right, to
literature. He himself apologises for supererogatory notes and
'would wish sometimes that they had been left out' – as Eliot
later wished with the Notes added to *The Waste Land*. But
sometimes, as everywhere in his work, he includes an interesting piece of information – for example, Henry VIII assuring
Bishop Fisher that suppression of the monasteries would but
take away their superfluities for more godly uses; and Fisher's
suspicion that the axe would go further – and be laid not only to
the monasteries.

Harington knew Dante, which was rare in sixteenth-century
Europe. He has an effective defence on the score of the bawdy
passages in Ariosto; actually, as a courtier and man of taste,
Harington proceeded by way of innuendo rather than down-

right crudity, though the age was crude enough in all conscience. And he knew people's hypocrisy: 'methinks I see some of
you searching already for these places of the book, half offended
that I have not made some directions that you might find out
and read them immediately'. As for bawdiness, what about our
own admired Chaucer, 'who both in words and sense incurreth
far more the reprehension of flat scurrility'?

In 1592 Harington was sheriff of his county and received a
visit from the Queen at Kelston – an expensive honour. In 1596
he published the book which brought him still wider notoriety,
The Metamorphosis of Ajax, a pun on 'A-jakes', for its subject
was privies. Elizabethans were addicts of puns; Harington, like
Shakespeare, was full of them. The modern cliché-reaction
against puns in general is rather silly: there are good as well as
bad puns; they form a traditional element in language and literature and to exclude them all is an absurd contraction of humour
and sense. Harington knew Rabelais, as yet untranslated, and
his book is a piece of Rabelaisian humour, though not only that;
it had its utility. It offers besides a good deal of information
about the age, 'this quick-spirited age, when so many excellent
wits are endeavouring by their pens to set up lights and to give
the world new eyes to see into deformity'.

He claims that he wrote his book to be talked of – and it
certainly was. It was published again by Shakespeare's fellow
townsman Richard Field, and was reprinted twice in the same
year before a stop was put to it: not on account of its subject –
apparently the Queen did not disapprove, but because of a
reference that was thought to reflect on the sacred bull, Leicester. The book is full of high spirits, its author's frank delight in
life and words and jokes, shameless and clever and gleeful.
Difficult as it is for us to appreciate much of Elizabethan
humour, even in Shakespeare or Ben Jonson's plays – though
there the action helps – Harington's is one of the few comic
books of the time, along with Nashe, which one finds funny.

Of course there is a limit to the amusement to be derived
from the scatological; it appeals more widely to 'normal'
heterosexuals like Harington or Shakespeare, or even Sir
Thomas More, than to the more fastidious taste of homosexuals

like Marlowe or Bacon. Everything about Harington is natural and normal, but also learned: shameless jokes about the Apostolic Seat, Latin puns about the god Stercutius or goddess Cloacina, discussions whether better to wipe oneself with a goose-feather, according to Rabelais, or tear a leaf out of Holinshed's *Chronicles*. Jokes abound about the Privy Chamber, the ladies-in-waiting and the smells that emanated from it; verses to the ladies 'at the making of their perfumed privy at Richmond Palace', his book to be hanged in chains therein:

> Now judge you that the work mock, envy, taunt,
> Whose service in this place may make most vaunt:
> If us, or you, to praise it were most meet –
> You that made sour, or us that make it sweet?

for the purpose of the work was to advocate the invention of the water-closet.

Harington argued that it would be a benefaction, not only to towns like London but to great houses and royal palaces, which smelt to high heaven. A couple of centuries later people said that Versailles could be smelt two or three miles away. This was the reason why the royal palaces had to be evacuated every two or three months, and the Court made a round at choice: Whitehall, Greenwich, Hampton Court, Windsor, Oatlands, Nonsuch. Elizabeth disliked Hampton Court, for she fell ill of small-pox there; she preferred the sea-air of Greenwich, or the purer air of the Surrey uplands. She was specially sensitive about smells, and the grandees close to her went heavily scented.

The marked increase in Shakespeare's sensitiveness to scents, after his introduction into the Southampton circle, has been noticed in his imagery. We note a certain interchange between Harington and Shakespeare, besides their common acquaintance with Richard Field. *As You Like It* was written only a year or so after Field published *Ajax*; Shakespeare may have picked up the name Jacques from it, for its supposed associations with melancholy, as certainly Orlando is suggested from Ariosto. Harington similarly has a return to an earlier play: 'for the shrewd wife, read the book of Taming a Shrew, which hath made a number of us so perfect that now everyone can rule a shrew in our country, save he that hath her'. Another exchange occurs at the end of *Love's Labour's Lost*, in the comic masque of the Nine Worthies: 'your Lion, that holds his poll-axe sitting on a close-stool, will be given to Ajax: he will be the ninth Worthy'. In Harington's collection of plays he had no less than eighteen of Shakespeare's quartos, three of them being duplicates.

As usual we find much unexpected information: about John Heywood, the favourite epigrammatist and writer of interludes, who got into trouble over the Six Articles. Henry VIII was persuaded that 'a man that wrote so pleasant and harmless verses could not have any harmful conceit against his proceedings . . . and so saved him from the jerk of the six-stringed whip'. Harington had no liking for Puritans, whose motto it was

> Down, down with it at any hand,
> Make all things plain, let nothing stand.

'They care neither for good letters nor good lives, but only out of the spoils to get good livings; our good lord bishops must be made poor superintendents, that they might superintend the goodly lordships of rich bishoprics.' Harington had been standing by when his good Bishop Still had had to deal with an irrepressible Puritan and told him 'Thou art a man, and mayest and dost err.' 'No, sir: the spirit bears witness to my spirit I am the Child of God.' 'Alas,' said the Bishop, 'thy blind spirit will lead thee to the gallows.' 'If I die in the Lord's cause I shall be a martyr', said the Puritan, irrepressible, incorrigible, insufferable.

All through the book there are laughs at various people and their oddities: the comic old dowager, Lady Russell, who would not even name 'love' without a 'save-reverence'; or poor Bishop Cooper whom everybody laughed at for allowing his wife to cuckold him; or the ingenious, but often absurd, inventor Plat, to whom Harington proposed a joint monopoly, of

Plat's artificial coal and his own reformed jakes. Of this last we are given a design, much like a modern water-closet, with cistern, tap, washer, waste-pipe, seat-board and all. 'To conclude all this in a few words, it is but a standing close-stool easily emptied.' It had been tried out successfully; but Leicester had made the objection that 'in the Prince's houses, where so many mouths be fed, a close vault will fill quickly'. The problem was indeed that of drainage, and the invention could not be brought into general use until the Industrial Revolution made piping and sewage disposal on a large scale possible.

Harington knew the great houses and their need of such an invention: 'I would appraise it in my house to be worth £100; in Wollaton £500; in Theobalds, Burghley and Holdenby £1000; in Greenwich, Richmond and Hampton Court £10,000.' Then, with a shocking pun in Latin, 'if I had such a grant [i.e. patent of the invention] my *heres ex asse* would be the richest squire in England'.

A year or two later his cousin, Robert Markham, was writing, 'since your departure from hence you have been spoken of, and with no ill will, both by the nobles and the Queen herself. Your book is almost forgiven, and I may say forgotten, but not for its lack of wit or satire . . . though her highness signified displeasure in outward sort, yet did she like the marrow of your book. The Queen is minded to take you to her favour, but she sweareth that she believes you will make epigrams and write *misacmos* [Harington's pseudonym] again on her and all the Court. She hath been heard to say "that merry poet, her godson, must not come to Greenwich till he hath grown sober and leaveth the Ladies' [at Court] sports and frolics". She did conceive much disquiet on being told you had aimed a shaft at Leicester: I wish you knew the author of that ill deed.'

Harington gravitated between Court and country, sometimes preferring one, sometimes the other; he gives many sidelights as to the former. 'It is a great honour of the Queen's Court that no prince's servants fare so well and so orderly, nor have more wholesome provision in all Europe. The stately palaces, goodly and many chambers, fair galleries, large gardens, sweet walks, that princes with magnificent cost do make (the 20th part of which they use not themselves) all show that they desire the ease, content, and pleasure of their followers as well as themselves.' Jesters were still maintained – the famous actor Tarleton was treated as a licensed libertine in performing before Elizabeth. 'That such kind of fellows as these be still hawking and hanging about princes' Courts and noblemen's houses is a custom so ancient that it is made lawful by prescription.' He himself was a good deal more than a Court jester, though an addict of jests and jokes.

He always pays tribute to Elizabeth's natural kindness and consideration, under the demands and duties of regality. In 1598 she was much grieved by Burghley's last illness, and 'saith that her comfort hath been in her people's happiness, and their happiness in his discretion'. She besought heaven daily that his life might be prolonged. When he died, she 'doth often speak of him in tears, and turn aside when he is discoursed of; nay, even forbiddeth any mention of his name in the Council'. In the last months of her own life he recalled 'the goodness of our sovereign lady to me, even before born – her affections to my mother who waited in Privy Chamber, her bettering the state of my father's fortune (which I have, alas, so much worsted), her watchings over my youth, her liking to my free speech and admiration of my little learning and poesy, which I did so much cultivate on her command'.

In his interesting discourse on play he favours playing for modest stakes, and cites the Queen's example. 'For, if her majesty would play at primero in that proportion of her estate as I have seen some of her mean subjects in their poor callings, she should play a dukedom at a rest [throw], and a barony stake – and then I know none able to play with her. But if her highness can vouchsafe to play sometimes with her servants according to their meaner abilities, I know not why we her servants should scorn to play with our equals or inferiors for competent wagers, as the loss may not be burdensome to them.' He realised well that the motive for high play – the Elizabethans called it 'great play' – with large wagers was pride, or, we might say, exhibitionism; for it gave the onlookers excitement which they did not get from play for small stakes.

He was a good psychologist, and knew how large a part keeping up appearances plays in society. 'We go brave in apparel that we may be taken for better men than we be; we use much bumbastings [padding] and quiltings to seem better formed, better shouldered, smaller waisted and fuller tight than we are. We barb and shave oft to seem younger than we are; we use perfumes both inward and outward to seem sweeter than we be; corked shoes to seem taller than we be.' We need not doubt that Harington was a dandy himself: he looks it in his portraits. 'We use courteous salutations to seem kinder than we be; and sometimes grave and godly communication to seem wiser or devouter than we be.' Harington had his own Christian morality: 'Labour to be as you would be thought.'

The year 1598 saw the outbreak of O'Neill's Rebellion in Ulster, the most serious challenge to English power in Ireland, which distracted the Queen's last years. Harington wanted to go, to get himself a knighthood – as Elizabeth later said; she was careful about honours, Essex, wherever he was in command, prodigal with an eye to building up support. Harington says that his Irish venture cost him not less than £300. He was not unacquainted with Ireland; like other West Country folk he had hoped to take part in a new plantation of Munster, after the devastation of the Desmond Rebellion (into which the poor Earl had been pushed by his fire-eating fanatic of a cousin, James Fitzmaurice). After three months' prospecting in 1586 Harington, like so many others, had given up.

Before going he received a letter of advice and warning from his cousin Robert Markham, which lets us into the state of mind at Court about Essex's appointment as Lord Deputy. 'Observe the man who commandeth, and yet is commanded himself; he goeth not forth to serve the Queen's realm but to humour his own revenge.' As for the Queen, 'we know not what to think hereof. She hath, in all outward semblance, placed confidence in the man who so lately sought other treatment at her hands; we do sometimes think one way, and sometimes another.'

Markham cautions his kinsman as to his conduct: 'you stand

well in her highness' love . . . mark my counsel in this matter: I doubt not your valour nor your labour, but that damnable uncovered honesty will mar your fortunes. Be heedful of your bearings; speak not your mind to all you meet. As you love yourself, the Queen, and me, discover not these matters. . . . You are to take account of all that passes in your expedition, and keep journal thereof, unknown to any in the company. This will be expected of you. I have reasons to give for this order: if the Lord Deputy performs in the field what he hath promised in the Council, all will be well.' As we know, he did not: all went very ill. 'I say, do you not meddle in any sort, nor give your jesting too freely among those you know not; obey the Lord Deputy in all things, but give not your opinion: it may be heard in England. . . . Your counsel may be ill thought of, if any bad business follow.'

Harington took shipping from Chester, for we have a few lines to his wife thence:

> When I from thee, my dear, last day departed,
> Summoned by honour to this Irish action,
> Thy tender eyes shed tears; but I, hard-hearted,
> Took from those tears a joy and satisfaction.

Characteristically he thought in literary terms of faithful Lucrece and himself as her spouse going to the wars. He was not hard-hearted – everything shows that he was a tender-hearted man: what he wanted was a knighthood, which he had small prospect of getting out of his godmother.

Harington kept a journal as recommended and behaved discreetly enough by proffering no counsel; he got his knighthood, with a mass of others, and then committed himself personally too closely to Essex, as people were apt to do, captivated by his personality. Essex gave him a command of horse under Southampton: 'your service shall not be ill reported or unrewarded for the love the Queen beareth you'. Essex then added a boastful postscript which boded ill for success: 'I have beaten Knollys and Mountjoy in the Council, and by God I will beat Tyrone in the field; for nothing worthy her Majesty's honour hath yet been achieved.' Nor was it by him.

Harington's cousin, Sir Griffin Markham, was given a command in Connaught, and thither Harington went, for Sir Griffin's sake 'and three Markhams more' – these had all given themselves, heart and soul, to Essex. While the Lord Deputy went off into the far west, instead of tackling the arch-rebel, Harington actually had an interview with Tyrone along with Sir William Warren. He fell for the great O'Neill's charm, who presented his sons, clad like an English nobleman's sons and speaking English. 'I gave them, not without the advice of Sir William Warren, my English translation of Ariosto, which I got at Dublin.' The Earl – a native prince to the Irish – politely expressed his appreciation of a passage he asked Harington to read, and courteously added that 'his boys should read all the book over to him'.

Harington has a favourable portrait of Tyrone, and was evidently seduced by Irish courtesy. 'The Irish lords, gentry, yea and citizens where I have come, I have found so apt to offer me kindness, so desirous of my acquaintance that my friends think it a presage of a fortune I might rise to in this kingdom.' A lot of people were apt to think that on first acquaintance, to be disillusioned later. Perhaps Harington's volatile disposition made him more congenial to the Irish than more austere English were, so that later he fancied himself for the Lord Chancellorship of Ireland, with an archbishopric thrown in. 'My Ariosto has been entertained into Galway before I came. When I got thither a great lady, a young lady, and a fair lady read herself asleep, nay dead, with a tale of it – the verse, I think, so lively figured her fortune. For, as Olympia was forsaken by the ungrateful Byreno, so had this lady been left by her unkind Sir Calisthenes.' This would have been the professional soldier Sir Calisthenes Brooke, who had transferred from the Low Countries to fight in Ireland.

Harington gives us snapshots of the campaign under Southampton's command, before he was summarily recalled by the Queen: she would not have Essex building up a party of his own within the state. Southampton performed bravely, but one

day Lord Grey refused to carry out his command and for this
was imprisoned for a night – an unforgivable offence to a proud
peer's honour. This led to an envenomed feud between the two,
challenges and a duel, and played its part in inciting to Essex's
rebellion.[2] Harington, who must have made a very unprofes-
sional soldier, took the opportunity to give the young Baron of
Dungannon an Ariosto, and to pay tribute to 'her Majesty's
gracious providings for us her captains and our soldiers in
summer heats and winter colds, in hunger and thirst, for our
backs and our bellies'. This was wise of him – though it was all
wasted by Essex's fiasco of a campaign – and it was not so wise
of him to accompany Essex on his precipitate return to the
Queen, after his futile truce with Tyrone.

All her suspicions were confirmed by the upshot, and she was
enraged by the loss and the cost, as well as treating with one
whom she regarded as a traitor, her most dangerous opponent.
When Harington ventured into her presence, she stormed,
'What, did the fool bring you too? Go back to your business!'
She betrayed the root of her concern in her outburst: 'By God's
son, I am no queen: this man is above me.' This was it: she
could never bring Essex into due subjection, the place which his
step-father, Leicester, had been content to occupy. Harington
was ordered off home; he went, he said, as if all the Irish rebels
had been at his heels. There he stayed in the country, wishing
that he had never been knighted, and consoling himself by reading Petrarch and Ariosto. This rustication was fortunate, for it
kept him out of the supreme folly of Essex's Rebellion.

This disaster, and the necessity of his execution – Essex confessed that Elizabeth would never be safe on her throne so long
as he lived – darkened the last two years of her reign. When
Harington at last ventured back to Court he was at first well
received; but 'she is quite disfavoured and unattired, and these
troubles waste her much. . . . She walks much in her Privy
Chamber and stamps with her feet at ill news, and thrusts her
rusty sword at times into the arras in great rage. My Lord
Buckhurst is much with her, and few else since the City business [Essex's outbreak]; the dangers are over, and yet she
always keeps a sword at her side.' She had gone off her food.

Buckhurst was the new Lord Treasurer: she spent much time with him over the cost of the Irish war and the drain it was upon the Crown's diminishing resources. Then Buckhurst brought a sharp message: 'Go tell that witty fellow, my godson, to get home: it is no season now to fool it here.'

One of the many grievances Elizabeth had against Essex was that, whenever she gave him a command, he devalued the order of knighthood by too many creations. After the Irish fiasco, angry and suspicious, she considered demoting them all. Harington wrote Cecil a characteristic letter about this when at Court in June 1600, a typical combination of waggishness, scholarship and good sense. He argued against any such proclamation, comparing it with baptism and the agreement of the learned that the rite could not be annulled – in other words, the sacrament was indelible. Speaking practically, the proclamation was expected immediately after Essex's return: that would have been the time for it, if at all. Now too late, it would give grave offence to many loyal subjects, and especially to their ladies, 'who are not yet so good philosophers as to neglect honour'. The proclamation might 'at least have a proviso that the ladies may still hold their places'.

The idea was seen to be impracticable and was dropped. But Essex knights were rather devalued: a contemporary saying about 'a knight of Cales', i.e. those created at Cadiz, being held cheap shows what people thought at the time.

A far more important subject that dominated politics – and was also involved in the struggle with Essex – was that regarding the succession, upon the Queen's expected death. Harington wrote a tract upon it at this time, though it was not for publication. Father Parsons' egregious intervention with his *Conference* (under the pseudonym of Doleman), arguing for the Spanish Infanta already established in the southern Netherlands, had created a stir, though his argument appealed only to his extreme wing of Catholic opinion. Harington easily confuted this, arguing in turn with both Papists and Puritans (Essex appealed to both), and putting forward the sensible, middle-of-the-road case for the obvious candidate, James of Scotland, with whom the unity of the island would be at last achieved. There could be no better candidate, or solution of the secular problem between the two countries.

Because of Harington's comic writings, his jokes and waggish sayings, his underlying good sense was disregarded (as by Lytton Strachey). Regarded as a light-weight and indiscreet, he was never given any job. That turned out to be a good thing: it left him free for his writing, by which he is remembered. Who remembers the thousands of inferiors who have held government jobs – except the greatest who have made history? Creighton saw the point and appreciated the good sense of Harington's tract: 'it argues in turn with Protestants, Puritans and Papists, and makes good the writer's case by appeals to authorities whom each class will recognise as above suspicion. . . . But its interest lies not so much in its main argument as in the survey which it takes of the religious question in England from the point of view of a shrewd man of the world.' In short, Harington was a sensible Anglican.

Harington had already made interest with James of Scotland by sending him his Ariosto. That very well-read young monarch had replied kindly, paying tribute to 'the worthiness of your good spirit which we account much of, respecting the present rarity of such within this Isle' – James was better acquainted with the northern than the southern half of it. The compliment he intended for Harington was more than generously returned in the portrait of James depicted in the book. What is chiefly remarkable is the mildness and catholicity of its tone. The egregious Puritan Peter Wentworth is treated more politely than he deserved. Even Father Parsons receives a compliment – on his prose style; but if the Jesuits want toleration, then they should cease their intolerable meddling with state affairs which provoked the rigour of the law against them, contrary to the Queen's wishes and some of the Council. It was Parliament, of course, that drove it on.

Harington approved the sentiment of the leading Councillor through the religious changes of mid-century: 'the Communion is good, and the Mass is good; they be both good. 'Tis pity we should fall out about them.' Why indeed? Harington was not in favour of the severity of the laws against Catholics: 'the sword is no good decider of questions in religion'. He was amused by the case of the two Reynolds brothers at Oxford, one a Protestant, the other a Catholic: each of whom convinced the other, so that the former Catholic became a Puritanical head of an Oxford college, the former Protestant an exile and professor in the college at Rheims. So much for people's 'convictions', each as silly as the other.

We are more amused by Harington's digressions and asides. He had borrowed Parsons' book on the succession from an Irish knight in Dublin; prohibited in England, it was dedicated to Essex – a provocation in itself, for it raised suspicion against him. Harington notes Parsons' strictures upon the House of York, not only for its cruelty to the sainted Henry VI but for its cruelties within itself – murdering a brother in Clarence and then making away with Edward IV's sons. Not for nothing was Henry VIII a grandson of Edward IV: he was a Yorkist in his proclivities. Elizabeth I turned after her wise and humane grandfather, Henry VII; again it is interesting that Harington thought that there was some physical indisposition on her part to marriage. He was in the best position to know.

His last visit to the Queen took place when she was visibly failing; his account of it to his wife, 'Sweet Mall', gives us a famous close-up. 'It was not many days since I was bidden to her presence, and found her in most pitiable state. She bade the Archbishop ask me if I had seen Tyrone? I replied that I had seen him with the Lord Deputy. She looked up with much choler [agitation] and grief in her countenance, and said, "Oh, now it mindeth me that you was *one* who saw this man *elsewhere*." And hereat she dropped a tear and smote her bosom. She held in her hand a golden cup, which she often put to her lips, but in sooth her heart seemeth too full to lack more filling. . . .

'Her Majesty inquired of some matters which I had written, and I was not unmindful to feed her humour and read some verses. Whereat she smiled once, and was pleased to say, "When thou dost feel creeping time at thy gate, these fooleries will please thee less." ' Here was the natural eloquence, the stylish gift for phrase, that had enabled her to keep people – and Parliaments – in awe. Then, pathetically: '"I am past my relish for such matters. Thou seest my bodily meat doth not suit me well. I have eaten but one ill-tasted cake since yesternight." She rated most grievously at noon at some who minded not to bring up certain matters of account' – as one sees, concerned for the state, her mind working, to the last.

He ended his letter pleasantly: 'next month I will see thy sweet face and kiss my boys and maids, which I pray thee not to omit on my account. Send me up by my man, Combe, my Petrarch. Adieu, sweet Mall. I am thine ever loving, John Harington.'

The memoranda he kept give us the best insights we have of what life at Court had been like in the Queen's time. 'I came home to Kelston and found my Mall, my children, and my cattle – all well fed, well taught, and well beloved. 'Tis not so at Court: ill breeding with ill feeding, and no love but that of the lusty god of gallantry, Asmodeus [i.e. the demon of matrimonial unhappiness].' With such cases as Mary Stuart, not to mention Elizabeth's own father and mother, with such ill examples as the Shrewsburys, Essex, Northumberland, Oxford at hand, the Queen one day asked Harington's wife how she managed to keep his love and good will. Mall replied that it was founded on her own steadfastness, her determination not to offend or thwart but to love and cherish. Elizabeth replied with her regular signature-tune, which was no doubt sincere: 'After such sort do I keep the good will of all my husbands, my good people. If they did not rest assured of some special love toward them, they would not readily yield me such good obedience.'

Elizabeth loved sweetmeats and tasting 'my wife's comfits, did much praise her cunning in the making'. Then – 'send no more, for other ladies' jealousy worketh against my Mall's comfits, and this will not comfort her'. However, 'the Queen loveth to see me in my last frieze jerkin, and saith 'tis well enough cut. I will have another made liken to it.' One is charmed by the exchange – and the naïveté. She liked, too, his 'merry tales' and the gossip he brought her from the countryside; while he addressed her with occasional verses, with special intention, ending thus:

> Let my poor muse your pains thus far importune,
> Like as you read my verse, so – *read my Fortune.*

She did not take the hint: she felt that enough had been done for
the Harington family already. If he liked to be extravagant . . . Hence his mercurial changes of mood: 'I have spent
my time, my fortune, and almost my honesty, to buy false
hope, false friends, and shallow praise.' He might be a Court
wit and a wag, disconsidered by the serious contenders for place
and profit, but he had no illusions about them.

> Who liveth in Courts must mark what they say:
> Who liveth for ease had better live away.

His life in the country gave him ease, and he undoubtedly had a
happier life than they.

No one has surpassed his insight into Elizabeth's temperament, or her politic personality. 'I never did find greater show
of understanding and learning than she was blest with. I have
seen her smile with great semblance of good liking to all
around, and cause everyone to open his most inward thought to
her. When, on a sudden, she would ponder in private on what
had passed, write down all their opinions, draw them out as
occasion required, and sometimes disprove to their faces what
had been delivered a month before. Hence she knew everyone's
part, and by thus fishing she caught many poor fish, who little
knew what snare was laid for them.' It was silly of a type like
Essex to contend with such a woman, who had ultimate power
and authority besides.

'Her highness was wont to soothe her ruffled temper with
reading every morning, when she had been stirred to passion at
the Council, or other matters had overthrown her gracious disposition. She did much admire Seneca's wholesome advisings,
when the soul's quiet was flown away; and I saw much of her
translating thereof.' She would keep Burghley till late at night
discussing the gravest issues; they usually agreed, but she would

sometimes submit her own judgment to his. Then she would call on Walsingham in private for his views. 'On the morrow everyone did come forth in her presence and discourse at large. If any had dissembled with her, or stood not well to his advisings before, she did not let it go unheeded, and sometimes not unpunished.' Thus, though she was occasionally taken advantage of, it was impossible to catch her out. 'By art and nature together so blended, it was difficult to find her right humour at any time. . . . When she smiled, it was pure sunshine that everyone did choose to bask in, if they could; but anon came a storm from a sudden gathering of clouds, and the thunder fell in wondrous manner on all alike.'

This was the way to keep people in order; this was the way to rule a country, as her reign proved.

II

King James's manners were much in contrast, and he had no style; but he made a good enough king, and Robert Cecil, soon to be Earl of Salisbury, had more power and authority than ever. The Cecils and Haringtons were old family friends, going back to the dangerous days of Henry VIII and Queen Mary. Cecil and Harington died in the same year, 1612, both of them only in early middle age; with Cecil's death we may regard the Elizabethan age as over: the Jacobeans came into their own.

In the last year of Elizabeth's life Cecil considered Harington a fit person to succeed Dr James as reader to the Queen. So did Harington: he hoped for Cecil's good word for 'such a place as nature, breeding, and my earnest desire make me think myself fit for'. Since nothing came of this, would Cecil make him Colonel of his county of Somerset? 'I hope your honour will not believe bare reports of my being backward in religion; for we have some pure spirited fellows that will not stick to say as much of your honour and of the best in the realm.' Both Cecil and he were moderate Anglicans, but Puritanism was on the war-path. 'I protest before God I am no Papist; I use the Book of Common Prayer, which many of our forward men do not. I believe twelve articles of the creed, and they believe scant eleven . . . though it is unusual in choice of a colonel to examine by his catechism. . . . The last 8th of February, your honour was eye-witness of my readiness' – that is, to serve against Essex's outbreak. He was lucky to have escaped 'being ship-wrecked on the Essex coast'.

Next year we have a fascinating letter which shows him, as so few, in the light of a connoisseur. At Stamford he had viewed Burghley's tomb – a columned alabaster six-poster, with the old man recognisable in effigy, holding his white staff of office: 'a most beautiful monument of his happy life and death. In my way thence hither' – to his house in Canon Row – 'I saw both the palace of Burghley and the paradise of Theobalds', to the latter of which Robert Cecil, the younger son, had succeeded. 'Though it were out of my way, I could not balk Cambridge, the nursery of all my good breeding', i.e. upbringing. He found the colleges increased in number, buildings added to and beautified, disputes between town and gown appeased by Cecil as Chancellor.

He had heard that Cecil wished to sell Burghley's wonderful palace of Theobalds, so he wished to see 'whether it were kept like a house the master was weary of. But when I beheld the summer room, I thought of a verse in Ariosto's enchantments:

> But, which was strange, where erst I left a wood,
> A wondrous stately palace now there stood.

The sight of it enchanted me so as I think the room not to be matched, if you will put two verses more of Ariosto to the chamber in the same canto:

> And unto this a large and lightsome stair,
> Without the which no room is truly fair.

I came thence full of delight, of honour and admiration of you and all your father's house by that I observed in this journey.'

Since King James laid wishful eyes upon Theobalds, it has not been realised that Cecil wished to get rid of his father's magnificent creation and was willing to exchange it for Hatfield. A connoisseur himself, he evidently considered Theobalds old-fashioned and wanted a free hand to create a palace for himself – which he did, on a quite different plan, largely of his own making. Since Theobalds became a royal palace, it was lost to the nation by the fall of the monarchy in the disastrous Civil War.

Cecil was an even cleverer man than Harington, and as good a letter-writer, if not so bent on being amusing. We find him a couple of months after Elizabeth's death writing to Harington that 'she was more than a man, and in truth sometimes less than a woman. I wish I waited now in her presence-chamber, with ease at my food and rest in my bed. I am pushed from the shore of comfort, and know not where the winds and waves of a Court will bear me. We have much stir about Councils and more about honours. Many knights were made at Theobalds during the King's stay at mine house, and more to be made in the City. My father had much wisdom in directing the state, and I wish I could bear my part so discreetly as he did.' He need not have feared: he had done marvellously well in bringing about James's accession so easily, and now he directed the state as discreetly as his father had done.

In the very first year of the new reign both Harington and his cousin, Sir Griffin Markham, were in trouble, the latter gravely. Markham was another of Essex's knights, the eldest of twelve sons of Harington's uncle Thomas; the family was touched by Catholicism and recusancy. A soldier of fortune, Sir Griffin was described as 'of a large broad face, big nose, black complexion, one hand maimed by a bullet'; he was fool enough to allow himself to be persuaded by crazy Father Watson into the Bye Plot against James. Condemned to death, his life was spared; he was held in the Tower, his estates confiscated. Meanwhile Harington had bound himself on behalf of his old uncle 'in his declining state', and found himself saddled with a large debt of £4000. His creditors were pressing, and in June he found himself in the Gatehouse, writing 'from my unaccustomed lodging' familiarly as usual to Cecil.

The overburdened minister was not amused by Harington's

light-hearted representations, still less by his escaping from prison. Cecil thereupon sent an officer to search his house in Canon Row, while another pursued him to Hampton Court. Harington protested in patronising tone that only for treason could a house in Canon Row be entered, and that it would 'be far from your course to lend your countenance of state to such a wrangle of debt. I have heard it noted in your father as a great note of wisdom that the second tale prevailed more with him than the first. . . . My escape was an honest escape: I shunned the plague, and not the debt. . . . I was strangely used and your name strongly abused.' And so he prattled on with jokes about one of his creditors boasting that in '88 he had £1000 in the bottom of a close-stool, and citing the friar who had been allowed to escape by one Simon, thus perhaps committing simony. And so on.

The minister was affronted by Harington taking such liberties, and he received an almighty rebuke. 'Although I have not so good leisure as you have to write, nor have so well studied other men's humours as you have . . . and have been taught patience by undergoing the sharp censures of busy brains, yet your advice to me to banish all passion but compassion was as superfluous as many other labours of yours.' Cecil had felt compassion for his old friend in his imprisonment and some sympathy for his escape, except that the use of his name 'proclaimed you to the world to have neither honesty nor conscience'. He was grieved 'to be exclaimed on in the world for being privy or party to such shifts, whereof my soul was innocent'.

As for his information that Sir Griffin Markham's mother had long pursued the Cecils with spite, 'it can no way move me (if I did believe it) to pursue Sir Griffin the rather for that matter – howsoever your hope of his land may move you the rather to accusation.' What a riposte, indeed! Nor could Sir John Harington hope to curry favour by dining out on stories against 'the late Queen of famous memory, as you are accused to do; for, if you know my sovereign's virtue as I do, you would quickly find that such works are to him unacceptable sacrifices'.

King James had already learned before he came south what an

incomparable minister the Queen had in Robert Cecil. Harington can never have received such a rebuke – in hopes of his acceptance of it Cecil promised, 'I will remain as I have been, Your loving friend.' And, in fact, the minister pursuing his even-handed course proper to his place – of which he was very conscious – took steps to end the matter by arbitration. In fact, Sir Griffin Markham's confiscated estates were bestowed on Harington – evidently in return for the large debt he had incurred on his uncle's behalf.

But next year, 1604, Harington was involved in another awkward dispute, with his brother-in-law, Edward Rogers. It would appear that Harington had often entertained his motherin-law, Lady Rogers, not without expectations from her will. His relations with his mother-in-law were more than usually ambivalent. A number of his epigrams are about her; some of them are kindly enough, others she cannot have liked, if she heard them. He reproaches her with a wavering mind, and with the unprofitable saving up of her wealth. The rich old lady would seem to have been addicted to will-shaking:

> If I but speak words of unpleasing sound –
> Yea though the same be but in sport or play –
> You bid me peace, or else a thousand pound
> Such words shall work out of my children's way.
> When you say thus, I have no word to say.
> Thus without obligation I stand bound,
> Thus wealth makes you command, hope me obey. . . .

Sometimes his mother-in-law would be angry with him; to pacify her he would read her a story, or – better still –

> Then you shall turn your angry frown to laughter
> As oft as in mine arms you see your daughter

– for Harington was blissfully happy with his Mall. When her mother promised

> But she should be executor sole, and heir:
> I was – the more fool I – so proud and brag,

> I sent to you against St James's fair
> A tierce of claret wine, a great fat stag.

The old lady invited all her neighbours to the feast, but did not ask Harington, who hoped for the best from her promise:

> Else, I might doubt I should your land inherit
> That of my stag did not one morsel merit.

This was just like his effrontery, or perhaps a better word for it would simply be cheek. And when Lady Rogers withdraws her affection from her son-in-law, to concentrate it wholly upon her daughter, he reproves her unblushingly:

> You then should love me first. Nay, never wonder,
> For let the heralds set our places down –
> I hope when Mall and I be least asunder,
> Your daughter's place is not above but under.

In Lady Rogers' last illness he was accused by her son and heir of rifling her house at Cannington, taking plate and money to the value of £5000, and burning title-deeds. Harington pleaded that he had gone to the house at Lady Rogers' wish, and there was not plate or money there to the value of £20. A Star Chamber case was made of it, and we find Harington once more resorting to Cecil, hoping that he would be present to hear the cause, in which 'I am defendant against my wife's only and natural (yet too unnatural) brother. A good fine may rise to the King out of it; for, if I be guilty I deserve it, though never worse able to pay it. But if I be innocent, as my conscience tells me, then a fine is due from a false and malicious and very rich accuser.'

He sounds innocent enough, and no doubt Harington's wife had some share in what her mother left. 'As the parties are so near allied, and at the suit of Lady Harington, sole sister of the plaintiff, the King's will is that the arbitrament shall be speedily proceeded in, with all regard to preserve brotherly love and amity.' Such was the King's will, and we hear no more of the matter.

We have instead Harington's account of his first meeting with King James – very characteristic and in marked contrast with those with the late Queen. 'His Majesty did much press for my opinion touching the power of Satan in matter of witchcraft; and asked me with much gravity, if I did truly understand why the Devil did work more with ancient women than others?' This was the kind of thing the new sovereign was interested in; with his homosexual disposition, he enjoyed a strain of misogyny. Harington 'did not refrain from a scurvy jest, and even said that we were taught in Scripture that the Devil *walketh in dry places*'. This was the kind of joke one could not make to Queen Elizabeth. James was interested in psychic phenomena: 'the Queen his mother was not forgotten, nor Davison neither.[3] His highness told me that her death was visible in Scotland before it did really happen . . . spoken of in secret by those whose power of sight presented to them a bloody head dancing in the air.' James went on about the gift of second sight enjoyed by many Scots, and named various books which he had consulted in the hope of attaining knowledge of future chances. Here the sensible Harington could not help him.

No less characteristic was James's wishing to recruit Harington's opinion against tobacco; he said that its use would 'infuse ill qualities on the brain, and that no learned man ought to taste it, and wished it forbidden'. On this subject the King showed himself very sensible. It would seem that Harington found himself in more sympathy with the intelligent young Prince of Wales, who tactfully pressed him to read 'part of a canto in Ariosto, praised my utterance, and said he had been informed of many as to my learning, in the time of the Queen'.

Mountjoy succeeded in crushing O'Neill's resistance in Ireland, where Essex had so signally failed; but what to do with the 'Isle of Woe'? While there in 1599 Harington had written a brief analysis under headings as to what was wrong. But people knew what was wrong: it all adds up to the fact that Ireland was a *different* country, a medieval and even pre-medieval Celtic society with inadequate attempts, with insufficient means, of the English here and there to colonise. The Irish could not, or would not, settle into the orderly ways of English shires, sessions, the administration of law and order, justice – they preferred their own disorder, like the wild Highlands of Scotland, the Outer Hebrides. No nice villages with farms and cottages and gardens, with squire and parson to keep order in the nursery. The most effective attempt was that to bring Presbyterian order and discipline into Ulster from neighbouring Scotland in James's reign – that at least cultivated the countryside properly.

In 1605 Harington wrote a more extended 'View of the State of Ireland', which he sent on to Cecil: 'you have been pleased in times past to read some discourses of mine, and to give them better allowance than men of meaner judgment'. It sounds sufficiently cool, and no notice was taken of his absurd offer of his services to succeed Lord Chancellor Loftus, with the archbishopric of Dublin to support him. Cecil had taken his measure; it seemed that no one took him seriously – perhaps even as a writer of talent, which he was: certainly not a politician. Creighton considers that he 'took a more generous and larger-minded view of the Irish people than did most of his contemporaries'. He could afford to, since he did not have to govern them; those who did knew how intractable the problems were and how incorrigible the people. Harington as usual rather fancied himself: 'I think my very genius doth in a sort lead me to that country.' No doubt there was a certain featherheadedness in common. As usual he displayed some sense in what he thought, and he favoured a conciliatory policy. But nothing would have done: the Irish were a different people from the English – it was the Counter-Reformation that had won with them – and they would go their own way.

The end of the year showed what explosive material the Counter-Reformation contained for fanatics, in the Gunpowder Plot in England. The alarm of the nation may be read in a letter of Lord Harington, head of the clan, who was very close to it, since he had in his charge the Princess Elizabeth, whom some of the conspirators favoured for Queen if they had succeeded in blowing the King and the rest of the family sky-high. 'What, dear cousin, could be more secret or more wicked? It shameth Caligula, Erostratus, Nero, and Domitian. Can it be said that religion did suggest these designs?' Well, the fact was, it did.

Lord Harington had taken part in the pursuit of the conspirators. 'I am not yet recovered from the fever occasioned by these disturbances. I went with Sir Fulke Greville to alarm the neighbourhood and surprise the villains, who came to Holbeach; was out five days in peril of death, in fear for the great charge I left at home [i.e. the Princess].' The fact was that the government did not know how far the conspiracy extended; they thought that a 'legion of Catholics were consulted, the priests to pacify their consciences' – the latter was true enough. Sir John was well out of it down in the West, but 'you will do his Majesty unspeakable kindness to watch in your neighbourhood and give such intelligence as may furnish inquiry.'

In the relief from the shocking fright he had had, King James received a congratulatory visit from his brother-in-law, Christian IV of Denmark, in an atmosphere of considerable euphoria: 'no lack of good living, shows, fights and banquetings from morn to eve'. One of the entertainments provided, a masque of the Queen of Sheba's visit to King Solomon, forms the subject of the best known of Harington's comic letters. 'The lady who did play the Queen's part did carry most precious gifts to both their Majesties; but, forgetting the steps rising to the canopy, overset her caskets into his Danish Majesty's lap, and fell at his feet. His Majesty then got up and would dance with the Queen of Sheba, but he fell down and humbled himself before her. And was carried to an inner chamber and laid on a bed of state, which was not a little defiled with the presents of the Queen which had been bestowed on his garments, such as wine, cream, jelly, beverage, cakes, spices and other good matters. The entertainment and show went forward, and most of the presenters went backward, or fell down, wine did so occupy their upper chambers. Now did appear in rich dress Hope, Faith, and Charity. Hope did essay to speak, but wine rendered her endeavours so feeble that she withdrew and hoped the King would excuse her brevity. Faith left the Court in a staggering condition . . .' And so on.

The entertainment took place at Theobalds. Harington did not fail to draw the contrast with the sober dignity of the entertainments there in the days of Burghley and his Queen: 'of which I was sometimes an humble presenter and assistant. But I never did see such lack of good order, discretion and sobriety as I have now done. . . . The two royal guests did most lovingly embrace each other at table. I think the Dane hath strangely wrought on our good English nobles, for those now follow the fashion and wallow in beastly delights. The ladies abandon their sobriety, and are seen to roll about in intoxication.' This was indeed the Jacobean age. It would fall to the King's younger son, as Charles I, to restore dignity and sobriety to the Court.

Harington was full of bright ideas; one of them was that the immensely rich Thomas Sutton, who was rather a crony of his and used to stay with him, should make his wealth over to provide for young Prince Charles, Duke of York, in return for a peerage. Salisbury had not discouraged the idea when Harington brought it up, and he went on and on at old Sutton with this in view. In the end Sutton wrote a disclaimer which constituted another almighty snub, if it reached Harington. 'I understand that his Majesty is possessed by Sir John Harington that I intend to make the Duke of York my heir; whereupon his highness purposes to bestow the honour of a baron upon me: whereof I never harboured the least thought or proud desire. Now I am going to my grave, to gape for honour might be counted mere dotage in me. This knight has been often tampering with me for that purpose . . . if he had had due regard, he would never have engaged himself in this business so egregiously to delude his Majesty and wrong me.' The old man had 'grown into utter dislike with him for such idle speeches'; he preferred to enjoy the 'liberty to dispose of my own as other loyal subjects'.

So he founded Charterhouse. If his immense wealth had come to Charles I it would have gone into buying works of art, and perhaps building more of Inigo Jones's great palace, of which we have only a fragment in the Banqueting Hall at Whitehall.

Harington recommended himself to Prince Henry, who asked him to write an account of his celebrated dog, Bungey, on whom he had written one of his many epigrams. This dog was certainly worthy of commemoration, for 'if he did not bear a great prince on his back', like Alexander's horse, 'I am bold to say he did often bear the sweet words of a greater Princess on his neck'. He could be trusted to carry letters from Bath to Greenwich 'and deliver up to the Court there such matters as were entrusted to his care'. Once, Harington's man Combe sent him back to Kelston with a bottle of sack in a panier on either side. On the way the cord slackened; so the dog left one flasket hidden in rushes by the wayside, carried the other to Kelston in his mouth, and then returned to fetch the first. Many more were Harington's 'merry tales' of his dog; until, one day returning to Bath, Bungey was more than ordinarily concerned to show his affection, leaping up to the horse's neck to attract his master's notice – and thereupon 'crept suddenly into a thorny brake and died'.

It was for Prince Henry's education into English affairs that Harington recommended Godwin's Lives of the English bishops, in Latin. To make it more palatable he appended his own accounts of the bishops, in English – and very palatable it is. It makes a substantial little book, not only full of gossip and good stories, as we should expect, but of sense and historical information. He had, above all, a vivid sense of personality, an insight into men's character and 'humours' – quite as good as Ben Jonson's, who had no very high opinion of him (nor of anybody else, though he made an exception for Shakespeare) – and a gift for rendering them. But he was a good Anglican, who had observed the progress of the Church of England from 'the hard beginning' to 'prosperous success'. He compared it to a fought battle, 'in which some captains and soldiers, that gave the first charge, either died in the field or came bleeding home'; those who followed had put their enemies to flight, and were victorious.

We cannot traverse his book in detail – sufficient to say that it provides a just, as well as sometimes amusing, gallery of portraits of these prelates. He had the advantage of being able to go back to his father's memories of the dangerous early days, of the plots that crafty Bishop Gardiner laid to entrap Princess Elizabeth under Queen Mary; of his father's imprisonment and his mother being sequestered to sojourn with Topcliffe. We have more about Elizabeth's personal characteristics, how she liked to be told that she looked young, her vanity over her singing, and how her sight had not decayed even in old age. Several instances occur of her well-known dislike of clerical marriage, and of bishops who lost favour on account of it. We have an amusing account of the awkward *contretemps* that happened to Archbishop Sandys, when he found that a young woman had been foisted into his bed by the host and hostess of an inn where he happened to lie.

All sorts of tit-bits come up: about the brasses of Coventry Cathedral, which had all been ripped up by virtue of a forged commission; of Ralegh's casting his eye upon the Naboth's vineyard of Sherborne Castle, belonging to the see of Salisbury, conveniently upon the road between the Court and his West Country. Harington considered that the money Ralegh subsequently spent upon it, 'in building and buying out leases, and in drawing the river through rocks into his garden' might have brought him a much better purchase without offence of Church or state. (Nothing now remains at Sherborne of these waterworks designed by Ralegh's enigmatic and scientifically minded half-brother, Adrian Gilbert.[4])

Harington's concern for the Church was not merely theoretical; we find him over some years lobbying his neighbours for the restoration of Bath Abbey, and before his early death he took practical steps for the re-roofing of the ruined north aisle. This was in keeping with the work of the Jacobean age in trying to recover some of the damage done to the churches by the Reformation, good works held up of course by the nasty, philistine Puritans. Harington naturally disapproved of these uncultivated kill-joys. In the last letter we have from him, to Sir Thomas Challenor in returning a book, he cited a local preacher who had quoted the prophecy;

> Henry VIII pulled down abbeys and cells,
> But Henry IX will pull down bishops and bells.

That is what they would have liked. Harington considered it a reflection upon his friend Prince Henry, and wished upon Challenor, 'having such place as you have', that the preacher 'should be bolted out first, and bolted in after . . . for these, not fools' bolts but knaves' bolts, shoot at a shrewd mark'. They did indeed; they showed themselves not only knaves, however, but also fools; for, though they won their war, they proved that they could not run the country on their lines.

Harington had had talk on these matters with Burghley on his last visit to Bath to take the waters. Harington was interested – as he was interested in everything – in the medicinal effects of the Bath waters. They were being sought after more than ever, and brought not only prosperity to the city but good company for Harington. On this occasion Burghley was accompanied by 'another cripple, my cousin Sir John Harington of Exton', later Lord Harington. The latter, head of his house, gave him a testimonial for his endeavours: 'you are not dead to good works, for even now this church doth witness of your labour to restore it to its ancient beauty'. He had greater success in the last year of his life with the Jacobean Bishop Montagu. The story went that Harington took him into the roofless church when it rained down hard upon them, and improved the occasion with a typical quaint joke. At any rate he prevailed on the Bishop to devote his revenues to roofing the north aisle, 'after it had lain in ruins for many years'. It was not the end of the good Bishop's work: he restored the neglected palace at Wells, and the episcopal manor of Banwell. When one goes to Bath Abbey one sees him very properly resplendent upon his tomb, designed by one of the Cures of Southwark and carved by Nicholas Johnson.

In the end, Harington – like Montaigne – contented himself with country life. 'I am now setting forth for the country, where I will read Petrarch, Ariosto, Horace, and such wise ones. I will make verses on the maidens and give my wine to the masters; but it shall be such as I do love, and do love me. I do much delight to meet my good friends. Each night I do spend, or much better part thereof, in counsel with the ancient examples of learning. I con over their histories, their poetry, their instructions, and thence glean my own proper conduct in matters both of merriment or discretion.' He had always found matter for merriment; if he had not always been discreet, he had yet made a good life of it. 'Otherwise, my good Lord' – he was writing to Lord Thomas Howard, naval commander and builder of Audley End – 'I ne'er had overcome the rugged paths of Ariosto, nor won the high palm of glory, our late Queen's approbation, esteem, and reward.'

He always had that exceptional experience to look back upon to console himself for what he must have regarded as the failure of his career. But need we? He is better remembered than the hundreds of conventional folk who held offices and jobs at the time. It is probable enough that he would have got some job from friendly King James, if he had lived the normal span. But is it likely that he would have added much to the written work by which he lives?

As a writer he had the good fortune to express himself completely in his writings – most fully in his Epigrams, which constitute a kind of autobiography. Family – wife, mother-in-law, as we have seen – neighbours, friends, rivals, critics, literary and political figures, all appear in the Epigrams, mostly by name. They are all the more interesting if we can identify some of those who appear under a pseudonym: especially, as I think we can, two leading figures, Paulus and Faustus. Even Creighton, who had the absurd Victorian disapprobation of freedom of expression about the 'facts of life', valued the Epigrams for the portrait of the life of the time they give us. We must not underestimate them as a contribution to the literature of the time either. Harington may be said to have answered Creighton and justified himself:

> Painters and poets claim by old enrolment
> A charter, to dare all without controlment.

Epigrams were much the fashion; Harington's were free and easy-going, like their author, varying in form, which was why Ben Jonson – who was supercilious about everybody except himself (and Shakespeare) – disapproved of them. Posthumously they awarded Harington his chief literary success; four editions appeared in the years shortly after his death, and all his interests are portrayed in them.

To those who know the time in intimate detail there is no doubt about who Paulus was; those who do not, of course, never can tell and their conjectures are valueless – as with Shakespeare's Dark Lady. We first learn that Faustus and Paulus knew each other:

> What is the cause, Faustus, that in dislike
> Proud Paulus still doth touch thee with a pike? . . .
> Besides, his manner is to speak in mock.

Harington knew Paulus:

> When you and I, Paulus, on hackneys hired,
> Rode late to Rochester, my hackney tired:
> You that will lose a friend to coin a jest
> Played thus on me and my poor tired beast . . .

Harington's relations with Paulus were ambivalent to begin with:

> Paulus, whom I have thought my friend sometimes,
> Seeks all he may to taint my reputation,

and this in his regular mocking, 'scoffing fashion'. For all his pride and scorn of others, he is himself for ever dissatisfied:

> But while he scorns our mirth and plain simplicity
> Himself doth sail to Africk and to Ind;
> And seeks with hellish pains, yet doth not find
> That bliss in which he frames his wise felicity.

'Rich Paulus' is an atheist, and this charge is several times repeated:

> Lewd Paulus, led by Sadducees' infection,
> Doth not believe the body's resurrection,

But holds them all in scorn and deep derision
That talk of saints' or angels' apparition;
And saith they are but fables all, and fancies
Of lunatics . . .

Harington portrays Paulus as 'a great man that expected to be
followed':

Proud Paulus late advanced to high degree,
Expects that I should now his follower be . . . .

That was characteristic of Paulus: he did not fancy equals, he
expected followers. But Harington was a follower in the rival
camp of Essex. It is already suspicious that Harington in his
prose says nothing of Ralegh, though they were neighbours
across the Somerset–Dorset border. A long epigram tells us
why Paulus is so much addicted to tobacco, and it adds a touch
to Ralegh's biography:

Thus while proud Paulus hath tobacco praised
The price of every pound a pound is raised.
And why's all this? Because he loves it well?
No: but because himself hath store to sell.

Whence does proud Paulus get 'those double pistolets,

With which good clothes, good fare, good land he gets?
Tush, those, he saith, came by a man of war,
That brought a prize of price, from countries far.

Harington had begun by being friendly enough towards
Ralegh in earlier days:

To love you, Paulus, I was well inclined;
But ever since your honour did require
I honoured you because 'twas your desire,
But now to love you I do never mind.

That too was characteristic of Ralegh: he required adherence, a degree of submission to his own proud will. That was not in keeping with Harington's essential independence.

Most of Ralegh's poetry – a whole class above Harington's, full of passion, pride, contempt, and himself – was written in adulation of the Queen:

> No man more servile, no man more submiss,
> Than to our sovereign lady Paulus is.
> He doth extol her speech, admire her feature,
> He calls himself her vassal, and her creature.
> Thus while he daubs his speech with flattery's plaster
> And calls himself her slave, he grows our Master.

Here was the rub: as Ralegh advanced in favour people became envious, and – with his temperament – he rewarded that with contempt, and did not hesitate to express it. Thus he incurred people's hatred, and became the most hated man of his time, and the most vilified. Harington reflects on his secret marriage, which no one knew anything about until I discovered the secret in his brother-in-law Throckmorton's Diary:

> One swore to me that Paulus hath a wife,
> Yet was he never married all his life . . . .

There never had been a public marriage.

So, when Ralegh was caught out in his never-explained part in the plots at James I's accession[5] in 1603, there was a universal outcry of execration, in which Harington joined:

> I have, said he, travelled both near and far,
> By sea, by land, in time of peace and war,
> Yet never met I sprite, or ghost, or elf,
> Or aught, as is the phrase, worse than myself.
> Well, Paulus, this I now believe indeed,
> For who in all, or part, denies his creed:
> Went he to sea, land, hell, I would agree,
> A fiend worse than himself shall never see.

This was the kind of thing that ordinary people – Harington
was not one of those – said about Ralegh. The identity of Paulus
is perfectly obvious, and unanswerable – as with the Dark Lady.
But ordinary people are imperceptive – as Henry James said
bitterly: 'Nobody ever understands *any* thing.' (They certainly
didn't understand *him*.)

Now who was Faustus?

The first characteristic Harington denotes is Faustus' super-
ciliousness about contemporary writers, and his preference for
the classics:

> In scorn of writers Faustus still doth hold
> Naught is now said but hath been said of old.

Harington returns with an ironical description of Faustus' high
descent, good looks and manners, his courteous speech, never
swearing or blaspheming, etc. Everybody knew that Ben Jonson had been his step-father's apprentice as a brick-layer, that he
was loud-mouthed, downright and coarse of speech, and had
killed his man. In literary matters he was very dictatorial and
condemned Harington's epigrams – said that they were no
epigrams at all, they were too short or too long. Harington
several times returns to this:

> Now Faustus saith, long epigrams are dull.

In verse Jonson took exceptional pains. He had been taught
by Camden to write his theme in prose first, then to turn it into
verse; and everybody knew the pains that he took in composi-
tion, the labour his work cost him. Harington:

> Of all my verses Faustus still complains
> I writ them carelessly. And why, forsooth?
> Because, he saith, they go so plain and smooth.
> It shows that I for them ne'er beat my brains

– as Jonson did. 'How Faustus lost not his labour' tells us:

> When you, fond Faustus, in an idle suit
> Had quite consumed long time in little fruit,
> Though you confessed you had your labour lost
> Yet you gained wit thereby, you made your boast.

A boastful type, Jonson did make a claim of this sort; and he had several times been up before sessions and had to give recognisances (bonds):

> Faustus for taking of a wrong possession
> Was by a Justice bound unto the Session.
> The crier the recognisance doth call
> Faustus, *Esquire*, come forth into the hall.
> Out, said the Judge, on all such foolish criers,
> Devils are carpenters where such are Squires.

Relations between Faustus and Paulus were somewhat queasy. Paulus was given to teasing Faustus, and Harington makes play with Faustus' physical characteristics: he was squat and broad, ugly and greedy; and what was worse –

> And in another sort, and more unkind,
> Wilt bite and spoil those of thy proper kind
>   [i.e. writers];
> Or doth he mean thou art a quarrel-picker,
> That amongst men wert never thought a striker?

Jonson was notoriously quarrelsome, and was more than once involved in affrays. In return for what he kept saying about Harington's epigrams:

> How can thy tale to any man be grateful,
> Whose person, manners, face and all's so hateful?

At length Faustus is found making up to Paulus:

> I find in Faustus such an alteration,
> He gives to Paulus wondrous commendation.

> Is Paulus late to him waxed friendly? No.
> But sure, poor Faustus fain would have it so.

This is borne out in the relations between Jonson and Ralegh. Jonson put it about that he had written a piece about the Punic War for Ralegh, who had used it for his *History of the World*. In return Ralegh gave Jonson the charge of his son on a trip to Paris; where young Walter played just such a trick on him as his father would have done at his age. He made the unwieldy Jonson dead drunk and carted him through the streets, displaying him at street corners as a more lively image of the crucifix than any they had. When the *History* was published Jonson contributed the verses opposite the frontispiece – but that was after Harington's death.

It is thought that the character of Sir John Daw in Jonson's *Epicoene or The Silent Woman* reflects Sir John Harington.[6] We need have no doubt who Paulus and Faustus were; realising their identity adds some strokes to the biographies of both Ralegh and Ben Jonson.

One more identification we may make. An epigram praises 'two worthy Translations, made by two great Ladies', both called Mary:

> Their learned pain I praise, her costly alms:
> A College this translates, the other Psalms.

The second was Mary, Countess of Pembroke, the first Mary, Countess of Shrewsbury, whose large benefaction to St John's College, Cambridge, made her virtually a second Foundress.

We need go no further with identifications, for many of Harington's acquaintance appear by name, from the Queen downward. Essex several times appears, once in reply to someone envious of Harington's Ariosto:

> My noble lord, some men have thought me proud
> Because my *Furioso* is so spread,
> And that your lordship hath it seen and read,
> And have my vein and pain therein allowed . . . .

Others of his Court acquaintance appear: the literary Countess of Derby, Alice Spencer, who married Lord Keeper Egerton; Lady Kildare, the Countess of Pembroke again, her brother Sir Philip Sidney, Sir John Ashley. Then we have his literary acquaintance: notably 'my good friend, Master Samuel Daniel', a Somerset neighbour at Beckington, where he lies buried. Both Davieses occur: John Davies the epigrammatist:

> My dear friend Davies, some against us partial
> Have found we steal some good conceits from Martial . . .

and Sir John Davies, author of the fine philosophic poem *Orchestra:*

> While you the planets all do set to dancing . . . .

Harington scores a point against both Gabriel Harvey and Nashe in their acrimonious controversy – very much a Cambridge affair:

> The proverb says, who fights with dirty foes
> Must needs be soiled, admit they win or lose.
> Then think it doth a Doctor's credit dash
> To make himself antagonist to Nashe.

Among West Country writers occur Somerset Tom Coryate, and the Cornish epigrammatist Charles Fitzgeoffrey; among neighbours, Sir Hugh Portman, Sir Maurice Berkeley of beautiful Bruton, and Dr Sherwood, the leading physician at Bath.

Naturally life at nearby Bath is depicted in a number of epigrams, some of which are generic, others may be individual; all are informative and spritely, some naughty. It was said

> That divers ladies coming to the Bath
> Come chiefly but to see and to be seen;

but, according to Harington,

For as I hear that most of them have dealt,
They chiefly came to feel, and to be felt.

Or, 'of a Lady that goes private to the Bath':

Lesbia, you seem a strange conceited woman
That, though thy bed to many a one is common,
Yet private still you go into the Bath:
We doubt your beauty some great blemish hath.

Even in rustication Harington had company, and plenty to occupy him. Inspired by Bath – but he had long been interested in health and sanitation – he wrote a medical treatise, largely based on Cardan, *The Englishman's Doctor*, which, so far as publications went, was the most successful of his works: six editions up to 1624. Another side to his mind – 'divers et ondoyant', like Montaigne – is represented by his essay, partly based on his favourite Petrarch, 'The Praise of Private Life', which was not published till our time.[7]

In May 1612 there came to Bath in search of health an old friend from childhood, Robert Cecil, now Lord Salisbury. Harington, who had suffered a stroke, was carried in to see him. Both were dying: Salisbury in a matter of days, Harington in a few months, on 20 November; Harington was fifty-one, Salisbury not yet fifty. Harington's wife, his 'Sweet Mall', survived him by more than twenty years.

Perhaps we may end more happily, for so merry a fellow, by going back to his early days at Eton, and his farewell to his Muse there on taking his son to school:

Sweet wanton Muse that, in my greatest grief,
Wast wont to bring me solace and relief:
Wonted by sea and land to make me sport,
Whether to camp or Court I did resort,
That at the plough has been my welcome guest,
Yea to my wedlock bed hast boldly pressed:
At Eton now, where first we met, I leave thee,
Here shall my son and heir of me receive thee.

SOURCES   Sir John Harington, *Nugae Antiquae*, 3 vols (edition of 1779), and *The Metamorphosis of Ajax*, ed. P. Warlock and J. Lindsay (1927); *The Letters and Epigrams of Sir John Harington*, ed. N. E. McClure (1930); E. K. Chambers, *The Elizabethan Stage*, 4 vols, and *William Shakespeare*, 2 vols; *Historical MSS Commission, Salisbury MSS; Calendars of State Papers Domestic.*

5

Lord Chamberlain Hunsdon

I

ENRY Carey, first Lord Hunsdon – and from its foundation in 1594 Patron of Shakespeare's Company – was a first cousin of Queen Elizabeth I. Where she was a daughter of Anne Boleyn by Henry VIII, he was a son of Anne's elder sister Mary, but not by the King. The father of these two girls was Sir Thomas Boleyn, a prominent official at Henry's Court, Treasurer of the Household, his wife a lady-in-waiting to Queen Catherine – so the girls may be said to have been in the line of fire.

Sir Thomas was a rich man of considerable ability, much employed by Henry on diplomatic missions abroad. The wealth came from his grandfather, a London merchant who became Lord Mayor, and Sir Thomas came into desirable Blickling in Norfolk and Hever Castle in Kent. His mother Margaret was a co-heiress of the Earl of Ormonde; the male Butlers challenged the title, but in 1529, at the height of Henry's infatuation with the daughter Anne, the King created Boleyn Earl of Wiltshire and Ormonde. On the execution of his only son, Rochford, for incest with his sister, Queen Anne – we do not have to believe this, they were 'framed', in contemporary terms too familiar today – the title lapsed. The residual claims to it resided with Hunsdon and Queen Elizabeth through their mothers; and the Hunsdon family never ceased to press their claims.

The manor house of Hunsdon in Hertfordshire had many Tudor associations. It was largely built by Henry VIII, for whom its chief attraction was its parks for hunting, a refuge from business and the plague. We find Thomas Heneage – whose son was to become Vice-Chamberlain under Elizabeth and a step-father of Shakespeare's Southampton – writing to Wolsey in 1528: 'Laud be Jesu, the King's Grace is very merry since he came to this house, for there was none fell sick of the sweat since he came hither; and even after dinner he shooteth till supper time.'[1] This was the dreaded sweating sickness, which killed people in great numbers, like the Spanish 'flu in our time in 1919. Heneage added a post-script: 'This night, as the King went to bed, word came of the death of William Carey.' This was Hunsdon's young father.

For a brief period the King had enjoyed the 'favours' of Mary Boleyn, as he did, later, those of her sister Anne after her training at the sophisticated Court of Francis I. She was a much tougher proposition, whose determination to become Henry's queen rather than his mistress (she did not love him, and was able to hold out for her price) made such a fuss in history. Henry married off her sister Mary, when tired of her, to a young gentleman of his Household, William Carey – it was all, if not in the family, rather cosily in the royal Household. The young couple were married on Saturday, 4 February 1520, with the King present to grace the proceedings, for we know the amount of his offering on the occasion – one mark, 6s. 8d. It does not seem much, but no doubt bride and bridegroom were provided for.

Their only son, we now know, was baptised on 4 March 1526, and given the name of the beneficent (and omnipotent) King. So that the boy was only two when his father died. William Carey had been a gallant fellow, much to the fore in the jousts and tilts at Court, in his velvets and cloth of gold – and would have made a career if he had lived, with such favour and connexions. The King had thought of ending the Ormonde dispute by marrying the titular Earl's son to his discarded mistress; with Ormonde unwilling, the lot fell upon William Carey. A daughter of his marriage named Catherine, after the

Queen, eventually married Sir Francis Knollys, who was another of Queen Elizabeth's Vice-Chamberlains. We see how the cousinage that surrounded her came to be formed: Careys and Knollyses, Butlers and Howards, on her mother's side. She could show her affection for her mother's memory, and her implicit assertion of her innocence, by favour to her kin. Not a word about her terrifying father; but once a kind word about her 'good grandfather', the humane Henry VII.

Princess Mary spent much time in the moated house at Hunsdon; so did the boy, Prince Edward: 'would to God the King had seen him last night,' someone reported thence; 'the minstrels played and his Grace danced and played so wantonly that he could not stand still'. When, after the black decades of the 1540s and 1550s, Elizabeth came to the throne and the Careys were in clover, she gave Hunsdon to her cousin, to support the title to which she elevated him. It became his country house in the south, and the Queen stood godmother to two of the children baptised there: his daughter Elizabeth on 7 June 1576, and a grandson on 26 August 1584.

Little remains of Hunsdon's time there – only a vaulted cellar and an inscription over a gate 'H. H. 1593'. The house was rebuilt in Jacobean days, and the parish church contains the marble monument of the re-builder, the 3rd Lord. Royalists, the Hunsdons lost in the depredations and fines of the destructive Civil War, after which the house was sold and the family knew it no more.

In spite of what people said later, young Henry was not badly educated: he wrote fluently, in a simple expressive style, full of proverbs and homely sayings much to the point. He did know some Latin, and was a patron of music, as well as of the poet William Warner, author of the popular *Albion's England*. From quite early he had his own company of players; as Lord Chamberlain he became responsible for entertainments at Court, and patron of the most famous of all theatre companies – that of which Shakespeare was a key member from its formation to the end of his life. James Burbage, who took the initiative in its organisation, was Hunsdon's man.

Henry Carey married quite early, when he was only nineteen,

Anne Morgan, daughter of a Herefordshire knight, another lady of the Household. Everything shows that he was very virile, positively philoprogenitive; for, besides giving his wife seven sons and three daughters, there were interesting illegitimates, as we shall see. He sat in Parliament, as knight of the shire for Buckingham at the end of 1547, and again in 1554 and 1555.

His great chance came with the accession of Elizabeth in November 1558, when he was immediately knighted. The new Queen, after all the chops and changes – not to mention Mary's burnings – needed all the support she could muster, in particular those of her own kin whom she could rely on in the insincerities and treacheries of high politics. Henry Carey was always an honest and straightforward man who could be trusted, more a soldier than a politician, or even a courtier – though he knew well the ways of the Court. Not for him what his dramatist called 'Court holy-water', i.e. smooth flattery and disingenuousness, of which there were more polished practitioners, like Leicester. Carey was rather a rough customer, but no fool: he showed that he had ability, but above all that he could always be relied on.

The Queen recognised this by promoting him at her coronation to the peerage as Baron Hunsdon, with the grant of the honour of Hunsdon, with manors and lands in various parts of the country to support it. The whole grant, though lengthy, did not amount to much more than £600 a year – a minimum grant for the support of a peerage. Elizabeth was not throwing money away, even on her relations. If Hunsdon wished to better himself he could only do so by earning it, by holding an office and serving the state. This he proceeded to do, honourably, all his life – though not without complaint. He saw others advanced far above him – Leicester, for example. All the Careys were constantly clamouring for more: the Queen made them earn it from the offices she conferred upon them. Even so – for all his desire to succeed to his grandfather's earldom – Hunsdon never got a step further in the peerage than that with which he began.

They were always reminding the Queen of their relationship. When Hunsdon's friend the Earl of Sussex – who spent much of his inheritance in her service – was not provided with 'an earl's living' in return, we find Hunsdon writing reproachfully to Burghley that perhaps then 'Her Majesty would be as willing to make him [Hunsdon] an earl as others, although she has made earls of nothing, both without land saving of her gift, and yet no kin to her.' This was meant for the two Dudleys, whom Elizabeth had made Earls of Warwick and Leicester. If Burghley wrote to him of the Mastership of the Horse (from which Leicester had begun his ascent), Hunsdon would scant believe him, 'as his pap is made of the yolk of an owl's egg'.

The new peer's fortune was to be made out of offices and perquisites, grants of rights to export cloths or sell or exchange lands. In 1560 he got the office of Master of the Queen's Hawks, worth £40 a year; then the wardship and marriage of a likely heir would come his way. In 1574 he was made keeper of Somerset House – which provided a lodging for him in London. Gradually these offices accumulated: Chief Justice of the Royal Forests south of Trent; high steward of Ipswich and Doncaster; recorder of Cambridge; high steward of Oxford. But the expense of Court life never kept up with it – apart from his growing family and the large household required of his station.

In the 1560s Hunsdon was much employed at Court, on formal and ceremonial occasions. In the early negotiations about the Queen's possible marriage to an Austrian archduke, Hunsdon was sent to interview the Emperor's ambassador. Bishop Quadra, Philip's ambassador, reported that 'she vows she will marry no man she has not seen and will trust no portrait painters, and a thousand things of the usual sort'. When the Emperor died and an immense Requiem was put on to impress Catholic Europe, Hunsdon as the Queen's cousin was a chief mourner. Elizabeth fell dangerously ill of small-pox at Hampton Court in the autumn of 1562. On what might have been her death-bed she assured Bishop Quadra that, 'though she had always loved Lord Robert Dudley dearly, nothing improper had ever passed between them'; and she especially recommended Hunsdon to the care of the Council.

At the Queen's first state visit to Cambridge in August 1564, attended by her leading courtiers, Hunsdon was lodged in Clare

Hall. We find him much to the fore in the splendid tournaments and jousts, along with Leicester and Sussex: in March 1565 a tourney of twenty-four horsemen altogether, 'a good one as things go here', ambassador de Silva superciliously reported – though he confessed that he found the Queen's talk fascinating. It fell to Hunsdon to receive the Swedish Princess Cecilia in the last stage of pregnancy – a few days after she was delivered of a son; or to welcome the Duke of Alba's envoy, the Marquis Vitelli, see him unbooted and refreshed before conducting him to the Presence Chamber with assembled Queen and Court. Or again he was given the expensive honour of taking the Garter to young Charles IX of France.

But what Hunsdon wanted was a permanent job, something of significance upon which he could employ his energies and provide for his family.

His chance came with the gathering crisis in the North, which proved the decisive turning-point in Elizabeth's reign. In the backward northernmost counties the Reformation, which had been decided in the south, had never been accepted: the old Faith still held the people. Moreover their natural leaders were their feudal lords: it was said that Northumberland knew no king but a Percy. Percies, Nevilles (the Westmorland family), Dacres were all Catholics. Mary Queen of Scots, having made a mess of her own affairs, arrived in England in 1568, to become the centre of all opposition hopes to the new deal, and make endless trouble. Though her brother, the illegitimate Murray, was Regent for the child James VI, the issue in Scotland was by no means settled; Mary had her supporters between Edinburgh and the Border, in particular the Kers and Scotts led by Buccleuch. The Borders enjoyed a state of society like the Balkans earlier in our time, or the Rif in Morocco: constant cattle-raiding on both sides, feuds, vendettas, burning of houses and peel-towers, mutual killings and slaughter – all celebrated in their barbaric ballads.

Scotland was a foreign kingdom with its own institutions, but the English could no more afford to let it come under a foreign power – France or Spain – than it could Ireland. At this time the fortifications of Berwick were rising, designed by

Italian military engineers: they still mostly remain, the best example of a late-16th century fortified town that remains anywhere, along with Lucca.[2] Berwick was the key strong-point that locked the Eastern Marches of the Border, as Carlisle was on the West. It was necessary to have a thoroughly reliable man in this key-post, a Protestant completely committed to the new deal, as Hunsdon was.

He was made Governor of Berwick and Warden of the East Marches. For nearly the next twenty years, in this most responsible position, the State Papers are full of his correspondence: his reports on Scottish affairs, sometimes missions or raids into Scotland; the state of the Borders, where disorder was endemic, and he needed to regulate it in accordance with Border custom and ordinances with his opposite numbers, the Scottish Wardens; the trials and hanging-up of thieves in number; keeping an eye, and more than an eye, on the recalcitrant counties in his rear, all too ready to break out into open rebellion – as they did next year, 1569.

The moment the Hunsdons were settled in at Berwick, we find Lady Hunsdon writing to Cecil that her husband, 'bending himself to answer the daily troubles of the country, hath laid upon her the charge of his domestics'. At their first coming the household numbered a hundred, and everyone expected to be entertained. They had got their household down to forty, and it could not be lessened. Great scarcity prevailed. Would the Queen bestow some gift upon them to help out? Next day Hunsdon writes that he cannot blame the Earl of Bedford for leaving this office, 'for pleasure or commodity is none in it, and less thrift'. He could 'live as cheap in London as here', and asks that Norham Castle might be annexed to him, since Sir Henry Percy will part with it. Nigh two hundred Scots were dwelling near Norham – a security hazard; the Castle was in disrepair, the revenues of the manor in the hands of the Bishop of Durham, so that 'the Queen hath but *Nomen sine re* [the name without the thing]'. Next, in January, a frost threatened the bridge at Berwick under repair; he was fain to have it watched three nights and rose one night at 2 a.m. to bring company to save it – the men were afraid to stand on it.

The main wall of the new fortifications is 'marvellous beautiful', but why were the castle and the towers pulled down? (Why
indeed? They were medieval, of the time of Edward I.) A feud
existed between the Earl of Northumberland and Sir John Forster, Warden of the Middle Marches to the south; there had been
a fray, in which lives were lost. Hunsdon forwarded Cecil a
packet of intercepted letters to the Regent Murray, to let him
'understand how they be ready to go by the ears, for they are at
catch that catch may'. The Regent had paid a visit to the English
Court in connexion with his sister Mary Stuart's affairs – at one
moment Elizabeth was personally inclined to restore her, but
the Scots in power would not have her back. Hunsdon had
entertained the Regent on his way home and escorted him
safely over the Border.

Hitherto the Governors of Berwick always had various tithes
in Bamburghshire; but they had all been let out, so that Hunsdon had to buy corn for his household. Next month he had a
suit pending for a fee-farm of his uncle Boleyn's land and asked
for Cecil's help in the matter. In the end Hunsdon got the
keeping of Norham Castle; for all its disrepair it made a country
residence away from his garrison, where disease was rife.

Whether there was much pleasure or commodity in it, life on
the Border had its consolations: in these first years there Hunsdon took to himself a mistress, who produced a likely child
who made a good career and ended up as Bishop of Exeter. This
was Valentine Carey, presumably named for one of Hunsdon's
captains, Valentine Browne. The boy was sent to Cambridge,
where he became a Fellow of St John's; in all the Registers he is
described as 'of Northumberland', his parentage not given, but
his coat-of-arms bore a bordure as an illegitimate son.[3] His
mother has not hitherto been recognised. However, reading
back from the good Bishop's will years later, we discover that
she bore the name of Hodson; for he left bequests to both sides
of his family. To Hunsdon's grandson and granddaughter,
therefore a nephew and niece, to the one £20 for a ring and
books, to the other £40 for plate. Larger bequests followed to
his mother's children: 'to every child of my brother John Hodson and to every child of my sister Veghelman, £40 each – in the

hands of Sir Robert and Mr John Jackson of Berwick in trust till they are twenty-one. To my sister Lawson at Bury St Edmunds, 100 marks – or to her children if she is dead.' (The Bishop evidently did not know whether this sister was alive or not.)

Anyhow that little problem is now solved.

In February 1569 Hunsdon wrote to the Queen personally about the needs of Berwick – the garrison were a scratch force. In April she wrote back commending him for aiding the Scottish Regent Murray to chastise Liddesdale, for ever up in arms. She herself was now facing the most complex crisis of her reign. Her cousin, the Duke of Norfolk, proposed to solve the problem of the succession by marrying Mary Queen of Scots; he was a Protestant, but that would prove no difficulty for her. He had with him a majority of her Council: Catholics like Arundel, and the aristocrats who were Protestant but hated the new deal or were envious of Cecil, who was its incarnation. Even Leicester and Sir Nicholas Throckmorton were against him, out of envy. If the Queen and Cecil had not held together throughout the crisis they might not have won through. She said that a month after such a marriage she would be inside the Tower – and she had been there before, under her sister; she swore Norfolk on his allegiance not to proceed. Instead of that, he wrote to Murray that summer that he was so far advanced in negotiation that he could not retract. He raised money from the Papal banker, Ridolfi, to advance to the Earl of Northumberland, ready to rise in rebellion, and to Mary; he was in touch with Alba, now arrived in the Netherlands to suppress their revolt and to give aid and comfort to Elizabeth's rebels.

In September Hunsdon reported that all Mary Queen of Scots' party in Scotland put out that the marriage was concluded, 'wherein they are in such jollity as who but they'. Towards the end of the year the Earls of Northumberland and Westmorland broke into open rebellion, calling with success upon the Catholic gentry, their tenantry and their feudal levies. Mass was said once more in Durham Cathedral; Barnard Castle was captured; an army under Sussex had to be sent north, Hunsdon serving under him. The rebellion was suppressed with much severity, but the two Earls escaped into Scotland. Hunsdon reported that all Scotland was against Northumberland's surrender, while his whole county was in sympathy with him. The Queen ordered Hunsdon to aid Regent Murray in rounding up her rebels who were fostered across the Border. The next thing was that the Regent was assassinated at Linlithgow; Mary Stuart rewarded her brother's assassin, who escaped to France.

Scotland was in commotion, and Hunsdon urged that the lack of decision regarding Mary was at the back of it. For the Scots felt sure that she would be freed and did not know what course to take. Westmorland put it about that Mary would be sent home at this juncture and Norfolk, now under house-arrest, would be released. Westmorland with Scottish support was raiding into the Middle March as far as Morpeth with three hundred horse. Hunsdon had sent reinforcements to Wark Castle, but no gunpowder was left at Newcastle, it having been expended against the rebels. He complained that it was the courtiers, far from the scene of action, who were granted their lands and goods.

The Papacy now – too late – sought to give aid and comfort by issuing its Bull of Deposition and Excommunication, which served best to whip up Protestant morale. The Queen wept to the French ambassador to think that her decade of lenity in rule should have been so ill-rewarded: the rebellion had broken the record of peace and quiet. Henceforth the issue would be clear: in a good many parishes mass-vestments had been preserved for yet another turn in religion; it never came, and they were at length sold off.

Cecil astutely tried to buy off Norfolk by agreeing to the marriage of his three sons to the three daughters and co-heiresses of Lord Dacre. This brought out the nephew, Leonard Dacre, in rebellion claiming the succession. He seized Greystoke Castle and fortified Naworth. He 'gathered together three thousand of the rank-riders of the Border, and others which were devoted to the name of Dacre: which, in that tract, was a name of great reputation'. In February 1570 Hunsdon advanced upon Naworth with a small force, but found it too strong to

take. He made for Carlisle to join forces with Lord Scrope,
Warden of the West Marches. Leonard Dacre followed, where,
upon the river bank, 'his footmen gave the proudest charge
upon my shot that ever I saw', reported Hunsdon. 'Leonard
Dacre, being with his horsemen, was the first man that flew,
like a tall gentleman; and never looked behind him, as I think,
till he was in Liddesdale. And yet one of my company had him
by the arm and, if he had not been rescued by certain Scots –
whereof he has many – he had been taken.'

Hunsdon had less than fifteen hundred men 'of all sorts' and
reckoned the rebels at some three thousand. No Elizabethan
suffered from false modesty, or underrated his own achievements in telling the tale; all the same, the successful action
against superior numbers made his reputation. He received a
charming note of congratulation from the Queen, in her inim-
itable style: 'I doubt much, my Harry, whether that the victory
which were given me more joyed me, or that you were by God
appointed the instrument of my glory.'

Nevertheless a chaotic situation continued in Scotland and
along the Borders. Westmorland was now with the Hamiltons
at Linlithgow, the Dacres and Nortons maintained by Lord
Home. Hunsdon had placed a hundred foot and a hundred
horse in the town of Wark, and received two hundred horse
from Yorkshire, but of very poor quality. Westmorland was
receiving succour out of Durham, where his lands lay around
Raby Castle. A French ambassador had landed at Dumbarton,
with the assurance that France could not in honour abandon
Mary Queen of Scots. (This was the crux of the matter politi-
cally.) No news of the surrender of the Earls: Hunsdon 'is yet St
Thomas of Ind [i.e. a doubter] touching the delivery of the
rebels'. He needed more money; comfortable words of relief
from the Queen were all very well, but 'whilst the grass grows
the steed starves'. He complained that he was given insufficient
credit – a regular note with Elizabethans: might he have leave to
come up to Court? It was not granted.

Instead, he was ordered to raid with Sussex into Teviotdale to
force the rebels' surrender; in April and May they burned and
laid waste up to Jedburgh; Home and Fast Castles were surren-

dered to them. Hunsdon's eldest son, George, accompanied them, for we find him issuing a challenge to Lord Fleming, of the French faction holding out in Dumbarton. A couple of years later George was sent on embassy to the Scots Court, and was present at the siege of Edinburgh Castle. Meanwhile Sussex had had fever from 'the extreme travail of body and mind with lying on the cold ground and hard rocks in Home and Teviotdale'. All between Berwick and Edinburgh were at Mary Queen of Scots' devotion, but the action had backed up the English party in Scotland. Hunsdon needed 200 marks for repairs at Norham – 'no place in the house was dry, the hall a fish-pool at every great rain'. He asked for four or five hundred trees out of rebel Swinburne's wood near Newcastle for repairs at Berwick. He had important business in London, and asked for leave. It was not granted.

This, he complained, caused him much loss – over his private affairs no less than in regard to his suits. So many obtained their suits while he was forgotten. The Countess of Northumberland wrote to thank him for his comforting letters (he was always gallant to ladies); she thought that nothing but death could separate her from her husband. She begged him to make intercession with the Queen for her children – and shipped herself off with Westmorland to the Netherlands. He reported that the bishopric of Durham – it was then a county palatine – was very weak, and small account made of the (Protestant) Bishop. Formerly Westmorland, Swinburne, Norton and others had kept up hospitality in their houses – now all void, that part of the country clean waste. The Liddesdale robbers were raiding daily as far as Bishop Auckland.

Though Hunsdon kept urging a decision in regard to Mary Stuart, one thing the crisis had decided: he was able to assure the leaders of her faction, now holding out in Edinburgh Castle, that Queen Elizabeth was at last fully resolved to maintain King James in authority and overthrow his opponents. He was now sent into Scotland as her deputy to treat with the new Regent, the Earl of Mar. He found that he had 'to deal with the wisest men of Scotland, and no wiser than crafty'. The difficulty of ending the controversy between both sides was so great that he would not have taken it in hand without assistance. The King's party could not subdue Edinburgh Castle without money, and Lethington and Grange would not yield it up. However, he secured the surrender of Northumberland in return for £2000 to the Scottish government at its wit's end for money. Negotiations continued at Berwick, where the straightforward Hunsdon found the Scots 'so subtle on both sides' that he asked that Bedford or Sir Ralph Sadler be sent down: 'a right wise man will find his wits occupied to deal with them'.

Meanwhile, at Court Cecil's daughter Anne married the Earl of Oxford; Hunsdon sent his felicitations, but it turned out anything but happily for everybody concerned. Hunsdon was upset that the Queen had publicly berated his son for dealing severely with one Carmichael, a notorious knave. His son had not deserved imprisonment or harsh words from the Queen before strangers, to his discredit; an old proverb had it, 'better for some to steal a horse than some others to look on'. What made the Queen so angry about this incident, we find, was that Carmichael was the Warden on the Scottish side of the Border, and this had repercussions on relations with Scotland. Next, Hunsdon repines, 'it has been an old saying, better a friend in Court than a penny in purse – which belike my Lord of S[ussex] has found', i.e. after his expensive services in the North. For Spain's interference in her affairs, the Queen had demanded the recall of Guerau Despes, without any further debate, 'for which he has a natural talent'. Elizabeth had sent Philip a courteous note of the ambassador's dismissal, with a diplomatic offer of 'continuance of ancient amity'.

Now Norfolk was to be brought to book. Hunsdon – who was rather humane, and wished Northumberland to be reprieved – wrote to Cecil his regret that Norfolk had proceeded so ill as to be brought to judgment. After all, they were cousins; 'but it is necessary to go through with him and the rest, for her Majesty and he cannot continue in one realm'. This was the crux of the matter, as with Essex thirty years later. Hunsdon 'would not willingly counsel her to blood, but sees that the preservation of her life and estate requires it, without which no honest man is sure either of life or living'. He was convinced that 'their boldness of her mercy has emboldened them to this'. He constantly urged harder treatment for Mary as the only way to peace in Scotland – her faction lived in hope of her deliverance. He complained that he had not credit enough to have his opinion asked as to Scots policy. That was no more than the truth. He had tried in vain to effect a reconciliation between the two parties, but he had not the political subtlety to appreciate the international difficulties, notably with France, in dealing with Mary. It simply 'passed his capacity to deal with the parties in Scotland'.

As for Norfolk, Hunsdon would be glad if his life might be spared, 'both for kindred, friendship and the nobility of his house but, considering what peril the Queen stands in, would renounce him even if he were his son. Unless the rest have their deserts [i.e. Mary] as well as the Duke, the Queen might as well let him live.' He was afraid now that the Queen would never marry, there are so many hinderers, whom God amend or send the Devil to fetch them'. He himself, with his straightforward mind, was in favour of her marrying the Duke of Anjou. He was sorry that Monsieur the Duke was so scrupulous about religion. Never backward in asking, he would like the marriage of Norfolk's second son for one of his daughters, or the keeping of Norfolk's mansion, Charterhouse, where so much of his incriminating correspondence was found (he was a most incompetent conspirator). Instead of that, Hunsdon got the keeping of Somerset House, with appropriate fee, as a reward for service. Might he have Lord Cobham's place, if the Queen thought Cobham not fit for it? This was evidently the Wardenship of the Cinque Ports. Hunsdon did not get it.

He marvelled at the rumour that Sir Peter Carew should get the Stannaries: 'an office of so many men should go to none but Queen Elizabeth can trust in – which she has not had at Sir Peter Carew's hand: belike *aliquid latet quod non patet* [something is hidden that does not appear]'. He simply cannot understand the Queen's refusal to decide; he puts it down to carelessness regarding her own safety. Indeed she confessed when Cecil's information came piling up that 'now she might see how convenient it is for a prince, yea the wisest [i.e. herself], to trust faithful known counsellors; and, if she had believed such, none of these troubles had been possible in her time'.

At New Year 1572 Norfolk was arraigned in Westminster Hall and found guilty of treason. At his execution he denied that he was a Papist; contrary to popular belief, he was a Protestant, a pupil of John Foxe the martyrologist – though much good that seems to have done him. Parliament clamoured for the execution of both Norfolk and Mary. The Queen hesitated for months over the first, but at length was forced to give way. She would not assent to the execution of a crowned head until her hand was ultimately forced; after something like a breakdown on her part Burghley and the Privy Council took the decision into their own hands, and Mary's head was off shortly before the Armada was on. Cecil had emerged in 1572 from the prolonged crisis, with the support of Queen and Parliament, his ascendancy recognised in Council, raised to the peerage as Lord Burghley. Though the Queen wished to make him an earl, he never would accept – wise man, to minimise inevitable envy – more than the humblest step in the peerage.

The new Scots Regent now surrendered Northumberland; in May 1572 the money was paid down and the Earl brought to Hunsdon at Berwick. 'He seems to follow his old humours, readier to talk of hawks and hounds than anything else, very much abashed and sorrowful, being in great fear of his life.' Hunsdon wanted to be 'quickly delivered of him and sent up safe as he has many friends by the way'. In June he was looking 'hourly for the discharge of Northumberland, as he has slept few quiet sleeps since he had him; as there is no strong or safe house to keep him in, he is fain to keep watch and ward round about the house day and night'.

Instead, orders were sent down with a long list of questions to be put to the Earl. From Hunsdon's report we learn much about the background to the Rising. The Council's division on the subject of the succession had given the opportunity; the Queen of Scots and Norfolk had taken advantage of it to make a *putsch*, backed by Alba and Spain, and the Pope. Northumberland had been 'reconciled' by Father Copley who assured him that, though it was wrong to rebel against an anointed Queen, it was permissible if she were excommunicated. This cleared the way to rebellion in 1569. The Pope had obliged in 1570, but too late. The Earl did his best to excuse Westmorland, on the plea that he was 'only brought to it by his wife, who was more vehement therein than any-other'. She was a Catholic *dévote*. What made all this dangerous was that the North was unreconciled as yet to the Elizabethan settlement. The Reformation had been made in the forward South and East, especially in London, not in the backward North, where 'I find the whole country, saving a very few, more addicted to the rebels than to her Majesty, as far as they dare.' This was what made Hunsdon's key-post at Berwick so vital; the Queen was reluctant to give him leave in the earlier years. It was only after 1581, when James finally settled for a pro-English course, that tension on the Border relaxed. Even so, at the slightest threat of danger – as over the execution of James's mother – Elizabeth ordered Hunsdon back to his outpost.

In July he still had the Earl on his hands; apparently the Queen was hesitating as to what to do with him. Hunsdon was not sorry at her change of mind, 'considering what loss she will have by his death and the circumstances how he was procured to the same'. He offered to conduct him to the Tower, though the country was full of his adherents, but he begged in any case to be delivered of him. In August the government at last made up its mind: Hunsdon was to deliver the Earl to Sir John Forster, the appropriate officer, Warden of the Middle March, to be taken to York for execution. The last words of the silly man on the scaffold were: 'I am a Percy in life and death.'

At last the crisis, and the strain, were over: the new deal had won through. Hunsdon was still not allowed to come up; but he meant 'to refresh himself in the country this summer' with his friends further south, chiefly at Brancepeth.

There now followed a *détente*. The murderous Alba was withdrawn from the Netherlands and replaced by a moderate and conciliator, Requesens. In 1574 the Convention of Bristol patched up affairs with Spain. Elizabeth was able to write Philip a sisterly letter telling him how thin she had become since the days when he knew her in England. Her diet was always light and sparing – a contrast with the full-blooded Leicester, who in consequence waxed fat. Elizabeth drew up a joke-diet for him, the wing of a sparrow, leg of a frog, etc. – not made public, as insufficiently regal; but it shows the friendly, affectionate terms they were on, nothing more.

Hunsdon was now more able to attend to his affairs in the South – though at the threat of trouble on the Border the Queen ordered him back to his post: on one occasion, with such a volley of imprecations and abuse as to alarm even the Careys. She had occasionally to pull out these stops from her father's repertory to ensure obedience: she knew quite well how everybody around her was out to take advantage of her, and gave voice to what she called 'the insatiable cupidity of men'. The Careys were no exception; she rewarded her kin, but not unduly, and for service to the state. When Hunsdon overspent himself, as all Elizabethan grandees did, and forfeited an obligation of £1000 to the Crown, he had to sell his manor of Morehall in Norfolk towards meeting it. Personal favour and relationship did not permit depredations on the resources of the Crown with Elizabeth, as it came to do with James I.

Perhaps we may look briefly at how this worked out in regard to the family. Hunsdon's eldest son, George, was knighted at Berwick, 11 May 1570. Member of several Parliaments for Hertfordshire or Hampshire, he was Governor of the Isle of Wight for twenty years, 1582 to 1603. As 2nd Lord Hunsdon, he was Lord Chamberlain from 1597 till his death in 1603. Since George had no son, his brother John, Deputy Warden of the East Marches under his father, eventually became the 3rd Lord. Lady Hunsdon had complained that she 'did not see her husband or her sons should be rewarded at Court, if they were not considered there. Here be askers enough, and nothing worth the having unrequired', i.e. unasked for. But they were all sufficiently provided for at Court or elsewhere. The youngest son Robert enjoyed posts on the Borders as Deputy Warden to Lord Scrope on the Western Marches. His fortune was made by his looks attracting the favour of the susceptible King James in Scotland.

Of Hunsdon's three daughters Catherine married another of

the Queen's cousins, Lord Admiral Howard: Hunsdon and he were very close in attendance upon her when he was made Lord Chamberlain in 1585. The second daughter, Philadelphia, married Lord Scrope and became a lady-in-waiting to the Queen. She was something of a gambler: we find her trying to borrow £300 from Sir Robert Cecil to repair her gaming losses. And, 'if I might be so happy as to see my cousin John in this rude centre, my love to my chamber [i.e. at Court] is not so great nor my devotions so much but I would find spare time enough to win all his money at tantos [i.e. counters]'. The Scrope son and heir was born and baptised at Hunsdon, with the Queen, the Earl of Arundel and Lord Scrope as sponsors. He was given the name of Emmanuel; but this did not prevent him from bringing the peerage to an end and liquidating his estate among four bastards.

The third daughter, Margaret, married the exceptionally intelligent Sir Edward Hoby, son of one of the clever Cooke sisters and thus nephew of Lord Burghley. The marriage was performed 'with all solemnity' in Maytime 1582; 'her Majesty honoured it with her presence for the space of two days, to the great contentment of Lord Hunsdon', and the rest of the nobility there. Hoby had intellectual interests, wrote a good deal and was a close friend of Sir John Harington, the Queen's brilliant godson. His wife gave him no children, but by his mistress, a Pinkney, he had a natural son, Peregrine. Hoby was constable of Queenborough Castle in the Isle of Sheppey, where he died. It is significant that these strategic strong-points were put in the care of the Queen's cousinage.

As with most of Elizabethan peers Hunsdon's outlay – a case of 'conspicuous consumption' – was greater than his income. In September 1575 the Sheriff of Hertfordshire had a writ to seize his lands for non-payment of £50, and also to apprehend son George, and nephews Harry Knollys and Morgan. This was awkward, because Hunsdon was Lord Lieutenant of Hertfordshire. Subsequently he became Lord Lieutenant of Norfolk and Suffolk too. These were quasi-military offices, and most of the work was done by deputy lieutenants; nevertheless they were not sinecures but very responsible positions as war with Spain

approached in the 1580s. Returns of all the musters, questions of
military equipment came up to him. Hunsdon was sworn of the
Privy Council on 16 November 1577, henceforth we find him
in regular attendance when in the South.

He favoured the Anjou marriage, and as late as 1579 thought
it best for the Queen to marry and have children – at forty-six!
Elizabeth knew very well that it was out of the question, but
prolonged the negotiations as long as possible to secure French
friendship against Spain. When at length it was all over, Anjou
was despatched with all honour, loaded with presents, accompanied by Leicester and Hunsdon to Antwerp and his governorship in the Netherlands, where he made a parlous mess of
things.

II

At New Year 1584 Hunsdon suddenly received a Court
appointment as Captain of the Pensioners, the small and select
bodyguard of the Queen, chosen from the good-looking young
men Elizabeth naturally liked to see around her. This was a
sweetener for service, something in hand for the future. It did
not mean that he was to neglect the watch on the Border, and
when he dallied at Court he received a rocket from the Queen,
threatening to 'set him by the feet' and give his post to another.
Walsingham reported to Burghley that the Queen's 'offence
towards Hunsdon rather increases', and in trying to qualify her
displeasure he had received hard speeches himself. In the invet-
erate faction-fighting in Scotland a number of Scottish lords
thought to take refuge on Holy Island. Hunsdon thought that
dangerous, and wrote in his forthright fashion, 'As Mr Secretary's [Walsingham's] course and mine are clean contrary, so
am I a mere stranger in all things.' The Secretary had ordered
son-in-law Hoby to Court at once, 'to go up for his pleasure
who, my son knows, hates him deadly. . . . So as, if her Majesty
will have him to come up for other folks' pleasure, he must take
post-horses [i.e. not his own].' Lady Hoby had only been there

in the North a fortnight – Hoby had sent his horses for her, now they were all spoiled.

It had been put about that Hunsdon's earnestness in Scottish affairs was 'in hope of a marriage of the King with some of my kin. I doubt not but her Majesty will answer for me therein.' In such a matter of high policy Elizabeth could always have confidence in him – as she could not in her cousin Norfolk. Hunsdon had received a writ to attend Parliament. Was he to come or no? This was 24 November 1584: 'the ways are yet reasonable, but if I tarry a fortnight they will be very sore'.

Next year, 1585, he was promoted Lord Chamberlain, a glittering position which made him responsible for much of Court ceremonial, reception of grandees from abroad, tilts and tournaments, entertainments and plays. Here, too , he had a Vice-Chamberlain to aid him, faithful Sir Thomas Heneage, who was something of a favourite with the Queen. In May a grand tournament was held at Greenwich, with a realistic skirmish; after which the Queen ordered a pause for the cooling of the fire-arms. Hunsdon and his son Sir George Carey, Knight Marshal, went down into the tilt-yard to visit the skirmishers, while the Queen sent down Sir Walter Ralegh with her congratulations.

Hunsdon was well equipped on both fronts for his Court posts, as a soldier but also from his interest in plays and contacts with theatre-folk. From the early 1560s he had had his own troupe of players, performing in London and all round the country under his badge and protection. Their tours can be traced in the town archives of the time, where these survive. At the end of 1564 they were at Leicester, and that winter at Norwich, Maldon, Canterbury, Plymouth – no doubt visiting other places on the road where records do not survive. In the winter of 1565–6 they were at Maldon, Gloucester and Bristol; and at Canterbury next year. At Christmas 1582 Hunsdon brought his men to Court, where they enacted *Beauty and Housewifery*. During 1582–3 they are recorded at Norwich, Bristol, Bath and Exeter.

In the City of London the Lord Mayor and Corporation conducted a running battle against the theatre-folk performing in the courtyards of inns – for all sorts of reasons, the inconvenience of crowds, dangers to health and morals, etc. When there was a serious outbreak of plague, as there was every ten years, they usually put a stop to performances within their bounds. It was for this reason that James Burbage built his two theatres outside them, the Theatre and Curtain; while later theatres, such as the Swan and the Globe, were built on Bankside, the south bank of the Thames. The chief protectors of the theatre were the Queen and her courtiers.

In 1583 the City authorities made a determined effort to suppress playing-places within the city, thrust the players out and even tried to put down the playhouses in the liberties outside. William Fleetwood, the lively City Recorder, describes the progress of the campaign. In June 1584 the Lord Mayor sent two aldermen to Court to obtain an order for pulling down Burbage's Theatre and Curtain, out in the fields of Shoreditch, where he and many of the early theatre-people and foreign Court musicians, like the Bassanos, lived.

When the Recorder sent for the owner of the Theatre, James Burbage, he found he was up against 'a stubborn fellow. He sent me word that he was my Lord of Hunsdon's man and that he would not come to me, but he would in the morning ride to my Lord. Then I sent the Under-sheriff for him and he brought him to me. On his coming he scouted me out very lusty, and in the end I showed him my Lord his master's hand; and then he was more quiet, but he would not be bound [i.e. give bond to carry out the order]. . . . He made suit that he might be bound to appear in the Oyer and Terminer [court of sessions] . . . where he said that he was sure the court would not bind him, being a Councillor's man. And so I have granted his request.'

Evidently it was accepted by everyone that he was Hunsdon's man, and this protected him. For the Theatre was not suppressed: it survived to perform many of the early plays of Shakespeare, until James Burbage himself pulled it down and transported the timbers across the Thames to build the much grander Globe in 1599.

Something of the jollity that accompanied so extrovert, out-

going and masculine a personality as Hunsdon's may be glimpsed from a well-known epitaph to a servant of his put up in
1586 in the Savoy Chapel:

> Here lieth Humphry Gosling of London, Vintner,
> Of the 'White Hart' of this parish, a neighbour
> Of virtuous behaviour, a very good archer

– one recalls the fellow in *Love's Labour's Lost*, only a few years
later: 'he is a marvellous good neighbour, faith, and a very good
bowler' (Shakespeare would have known the Savoy Chapel
well, and the company in the neighbourhood) –

> And of honest mirth, a good company keeper:
> So well inclined to poor and rich,
> God send more Goslings to be sich [such].

A Shakespearean character evidently, and a man after the old
sport Hunsdon's heart.

Hunsdon was already involved in a property transaction on
the South Bank, the manor of Paris Garden. At his request the
Queen granted the manor to Robert Newdigate and Arthur
Fountayne.[4] These last two released to Hunsdon the rights and
profits of the customary lands of the manor. Eventually Hunsdon sold off his rights, until the manor came into the hands of
Francis Langley, who proceeded to build the Swan Theatre
there. This is well known as the only Elizabethan theatre of
which we possess a drawing of the interior, the arrangement of
tiring-house and stage, upon which action is portrayed.

A mountain of mainly superfluous discussion has been
erected upon this – as also upon the next thing that happened.
Langley, like many Elizabethans, was involved in a hornets'
nest of quarrels and law-suits, in particular with a Surrey J. P.,
William Gardiner, who, in one of his writs of attachment to
keep the peace, in 1596, included the name of William Shakespeare along with Langley. That is all there is to it. The inclusion
of the actor's name is purely formal and would indicate that his
company – the Lord Chamberlain's – was acting that season at

the Swan. For we otherwise also know that the actor transferred his lodging in 1596–7 from Bishopsgate to Southwark.

Shakespeare was long and intimately acquainted with Blackfriars, for there lived his fellow townsman Richard Field – the two families had transactions with each other at Stratford – who printed his poems *Venus and Adonis* in 1593 and *The Rape of Lucrece* in 1594, dedicated to his patron, young Southampton. Lord Hunsdon, too, was equally acquainted with Blackfriars; he had a lease of houses there; his son George, the 2nd Lord, who became Lord Chamberlain in 1597, lived there. The Burbages were no less concerned; for in 1596 James Burbage bought part of the buildings there, which after 1608 became the winter playing-place of Shakespeare's Company, eventually more profitable and famous even than the Globe.

Long before that, the Earl of Oxford and John Lyly used the great house within Blackfriars for performances of plays by their boys' company. When Oxford's tenancy came to an end, his boys' company dispersed in 1584 and immediately Hunsdon took over the premises for £50 a year. It was reported that Hunsdon had bought the house in Blackfriars next to his son's, Sir George Carey's. Hunsdon continued his interest in Blackfriars to the last year of his life, for we find him writing later for a renewal of the leases. He complains that 'the tenants of the adjoining houses, having the use of the leads of the roof, suffer the boys to get on them and cut them with knives and bore them through with bodkins; and the rain coming through, to his great annoyance, he requests to have the use of the said leads, and he will repair them at his own cost'. This was in 1590. He already had an official London residence in Somerset House; one wonders what, or for whom, he needed this alternative residence in Blackfriars?

It was in 1596 that James Burbage bought a portion of the mansion within, intending to turn it into an indoor playhouse. In November a petition was got up by the inhabitants of the precinct against the project – it was understandable that they would object to the players' drums and trumpets and the concourse of people, right next door to the late Lord Chamberlain's and the new Lord Hunsdon's houses. His father had died in

July; the new Lord signed the petition, along with Robert Cecil's obstreperous aunt, the Dowager Lady Russell, Richard Field, Dr William Paddy, the eminent physician whom Simon Forman knew. The 2nd Lord Hunsdon continued to live in Blackfriars; it was not until 1608 that the Burbages were able to fulfil their intention and construct their theatre. Of this William Shakespeare became a part-owner, and later of a convenient half of the gate-house leading into the precinct.

We see how much Shakespeare was associated with Black-friars over many years, where his later plays were to be per-formed; and also that Hunsdon was a good friend to the players. Upon his death Thomas Nashe wrote, 'the players are now piteously persecuted by the Lord Mayor and the aldermen; and however in their old Lord's [Hunsdon's] time they thought their state settled, it is now so uncertain that they cannot build upon it'. No wonder they moved more and more across the Thames, out of reach.

We may resume briefly the peregrinations of Hunsdon's troupe around the country, referred to as the Lord Chamber-lain's men, though not yet the official Lord Chamberlain's Company formed in 1594, to become so famous. In 1585 they were playing with the Lord Admiral's men at Leicester, and during the Christmas revels at Court they played together. The Chamberlain's men are recorded in subsequent years at Coven-try, Saffron Walden and Maidstone.

Then came the catastrophic plague during two years follow-ing, 1592 and 1593. This marked a turning-point in the history of the companies, threw them into disarray and distress; some of them went out of business, one of them at least went broke (an Elizabethan word), others amalgamated and tried to strug-gle along together. Hence the confusion that surrounds the individual troupes and the actors' careers: for all the research that has been put into it, it is impossible to wrest clarity out of kaleidoscopic confusion. Hence too the crisis in the lives of the theatre-folk, the deaths in these dismaying years, which we can follow in the surviving correspondence of the leading actor, Edward Alleyn, with his step-father-in-law, Henslowe, the theatre entrepreneur. The whole family of Robert Browne the actor was wiped out; in 1592 died Robert Greene and Thomas

Watson, who both wrote for the players; in 1593 Marlowe was killed in a tavern brawl, and Thomas Kyd died; not long after, George Peele disappeared. That William Shakespeare came through was largely owing, as he movingly acknowledged, to his having found a generous patron in young Southampton.

Lord Chamberlain Hunsdon played a proper part as patron not only of players and musicians, but of poets. A much admired poet was William Warner, author of one of the most successful poems of the day, *Albion's England*. Though we may not respond to the fourteeners in which it was written, Elizabethans did: edition upon edition poured from the press all through Shakespeare's lifetime. It had its influence upon him, for it chimed with his own mood, responsive to that of the time, racy and vigorous, above all patriotic. Warner was a friend of Marlowe, and his long poem was praised by Nashe and Drayton, both well known to Shakespeare. Drayton, also a friend of Warner, has a judicious, critical tribute to his poem, which – famous in its day – was dedicated to Hunsdon.

Warner's collection of prose-tales, *Pan his Syrinx*, was dedicated to Hunsdon's son, Sir George Carey, the 2nd Lord Chamberlain Hunsdon. What is significant is that Warner translated Plautus' *Menaechmi* into English. It is well known that this was the prime source of Shakespeare's first comedy, *The Comedy of Errors*. Warner's translation was entered for publication in 1594 and printed in 1595. It has usually been held that Shakespeare read this play in manuscript, for Warner handed about this work of 'much pleasant error . . . for the use and delight of his private friends'. We see a reflection in the title Shakespeare gave to his play; the suggestion is all the more probable from his association with just this circle, and it serves to underline it.

Meanwhile we find traces of Hunsdon's activities and official employments in the State Papers. When Scottish affairs took a threatening turn with the arrival of James's cousin, Esmé Stuart, from the French Court, and their overthrow and execution of the Protestant Regent Morton in 1581–2, Hunsdon was ordered to reinforce Berwick with 200 men and call out the Border militia. The crisis passed, and next we find him in Antwerp with Leicester conferring with the Prince of Orange, the heroic William the Silent, the spirit of Dutch resistance. When the Spanish ambassador, Mendoza, involved in Francis Throckmorton's treason, received his *démission* Hunsdon was present with all the Council, Walsingham voicing the government's accusations since he 'spoke Italian more readily than the others'.

The Pretender to the throne of Portugal, Don Antonio, took refuge in England; when he fell ill the Queen sent Lord Admiral Howard and the Lord Chamberlain to visit him. We often find these two together, connected as they were by kinship and marriage. The Spaniards always regarded Hunsdon as a leading heretic – naturally, with his Boleyn background, what else could be expected? No smooth, disingenuous divagations in his course, as there had been with Leicester's. We find him engaged in the prosecution of recusants, as readily as in the hanging of thieves on the Borders. In 1587 Hunsdon, Leicester, Howard and Walsingham were at one in urging upon the Queen that Parliament would not vote supplies unless she consented to Mary Queen of Scots' execution. Elizabeth was hesitating as she had done over Norfolk, and was to do over Lopez, driven to death by Essex in 1594.

In the critical situation that followed Mary's execution – though James could do nothing about it and was now firmly aligned with the English in time for the Armada – Hunsdon was sent back to Berwick. In February 1588 he was conferring with the Earl of Arran on the Border, while in June – when the Armada was on the way – his son George Carey was in Scotland well received by James, who was now assured of his ultimate expectations of the English throne. Thus Hunsdon was free that tumultuous and tempestuous summer to come south and take command of the force that was to guard the Queen personally in case of invasion. For his services in Armada year Hunsdon was rewarded with a profitable licence to export 20,000 cloths in six years; while the favourite Ralegh was granted one to export 8000 cloths in four years. A little later there was gossip at Court about his testy words against the Queen making such knights as Ralegh and Drake – which other countries spoke shame of.

As Lord Chamberlain, Hunsdon was resident now in the South, and here we find many traces of how busily he was kept occupied with affairs great and small. As a member of the Privy Council he took part now in decisions of high policy – he was a commissioner in 1585 in the crucial negotiations with the Dutch that led to the Treaty of Greenwich and open intervention against Spain in the Netherlands. Burghley regarded his opinion as of chief value in regard to Scottish affairs. James had made up his mind, over the crisis of his mother's execution and the threat of the Armada, as to which side his bread was buttered. Henceforth he was reliable, waiting, if with gathering impatience as the years rolled on, for the succession to the English throne.

Hunsdon could afford to leave routine work to his deputies – his family were well entrenched along the Border. In April 1595 he is seeking instructions from Robert Cecil as to how his son, John Carey, should greet King James at Holliday Hill on the Border. The Lord Chamberlain would have waited on the Queen, but 'tomorrow I do begin my physic' (Elizabethans purged heavily in the spring). In the last months of his life he was involved, with the leading members of the government – Burghley, Robert Cecil, Lord Cobham and others – in the negotiations with Henry of Navarre's ambassador for an offensive and defensive alliance – advancing him money to prevent him from making peace with Spain. When Henry ratted on this and made the Peace of Vervins in 1598, this is reflected on in the oath-breaking allusions in the revision of that very topical play *Love's Labour's Lost*.

In smaller matters, the Lord Chamberlain had to deal with the lodgings of officials and visitors at Court. He writes to Heneage as Vice-Chamberlain regarding the title to stables at the Savoy – the Elizabethan version of parking troubles. Then Sir Robert Cecil himself lodges a complaint. Hunsdon assures him, 'I am very sorry that you are so ill lodged, but it is the more excusable because I perceive it was long of [i.e. because of] yourself; if the Usher had done it I should have been very angry withal. Now my daughter Scrope comes away [i.e. from her period of waiting on the Queen], you and your lady shall have that lodging. Let my lady, your wife, tell my daughter that I will her to deliver the key of her lodging to my lady your wife.' In October 1595 Robert Cecil wants a more important favour: Hunsdon will willingly perform Cecil's wish, 'if Mr Vice-Chamberlain [Sir Thomas Heneage] do not recover. Yesterday there was great hope, but today as great despair, for his looks are again very ghastly and his speech fails. If he do depart, nobody shall prevent you.'

The Lord Chamberlain was besieged by suitors great and small. Sir Matthew Arundell and other local landowners besought him as Chief Justice of the Forests to determine the bounds of Cranborne Chase. Philip Gawdy writes in December 1592, 'Sweet Brother, I have here sent thee down a brace of warrants of my Lord Chamberlain: if he had not had so many unreasonable suitors for them I had sent you more.' This was J. P.s' business in Norfolk, of which Hunsdon was now Lord Lieutenant. Next December, 'my Lord Chamberlain hath got the gout in one of his toes; he used me well and you very kindly. Sir Arthur Heveningham gave him a very big flying tassel [falcon], and was the most importunate suitor to be sheriff that ever was.' In February 1594 the presents sent up to the Lord Admiral and Lord Chamberlain – those cousins whose players played together this June at Newington Butts – 'were very highly well taken, and they were the first they had yet this year. I had many thanks and many kind promises.' Gawdy sends down the news from London to the country. 'Dr Lopez hath been often examined and divers times upon the rack; he confesseth all things very frankly.' In September, 'I am resident either at Court, or else continually with Don Antonio Perez at Essex House, whom my Lord [Essex] useth with high favours. Pray tell Sir Edward Wotton that Antonio Perez *beza la mains de su Signoria* [*sic*, i.e. kisses the hands of his lordship].'

We learn much more about Dr Lopez and also Antonio Perez from Anthony Bacon, Essex's secretary who had to deal with both. Lopez was the Queen's doctor whom Essex was hounding to death on a charge of intending to poison her; unfortunately for himself, Lopez was a boastful type who involved himself in intelligence matters. The Queen and the Cecils were convinced of his essential innocence: the latter found 'no matter of malice, for in the poor man's house were found no writings of intelligences', and they opposed his prosecution. Essex made it a matter of honour: 'I have discovered a most dangerous and desperate treason'; the point of the conspiracy was her Majesty's death; the executioner should have been Dr Lopez; the manner, poison. 'This I have so followed as I will make it appear as clear as the noonday.'

Elizabeth was unconvinced, and called him 'a rash and temerarious youth' – that only made him the more headstrong. The Catholic traitor Sir William Stanley[5] was said to have sent over agents to kill Perez; that was not unlikely, for Perez, as Philip II's former Secretary of State, knew all his secrets. Letters from the Conde de Fuentes tried to recruit Lopez's assistance for this purpose. On the rack the poor doctor swore and forswore himself, confessed that he had received letters from Spanish emissaries, but had answered only one in which he assured the King of his service, if only he might live in Antwerp. This was probably the limit of his 'treason', but it was dangerous enough.

The Lopez affair hung fire, through the winter of 1593–4; to force the hands of the Queen, young Essex whipped up public sentiment and residual anti-Semitism. In February 1594, 'great expedition was making to bring the affair before the public'. Anthony Bacon was employed to draw up the charge against Lopez who was tried at the Guildhall, on 28 February, with two Portuguese produced as witnesses, though no letter was found to incriminate him. No wonder Secretary Faunt wrote, 'this day's work breedeth much discourse'. Essex concentrated his efforts for ten days on the business, 'wherein, says he, he hath won the spurs and saddle also, if right be done him'. He then returned to Court to urge on the execution of the sentence.

Elizabeth held up the sentence for months, until she was forced by Essex and public clamour to give way. On 7 June Lopez and the two Portuguese were taken to Tyburn, where on the scaffold the Doctor somewhat tactlessly said that he 'loved the Queen as well as he loved Jesus Christ – which, from a man of the Jewish profession, moved no small laughter in the standers-by'. Thus was the shadow upon the Queen, the threat, as people supposed, eliminated:

> The mortal moon hath her eclipse endured

– i.e. she has come through it. William Shakespeare, as an Englishman of the day, took the ordinary view of the affair; and that this was the date of that Sonnet 107 is made doubly clear by the second reference:

> And peace proclaims olives of endless age

– for in May 1594 Paris surrendered to Navarre, now recognised as Henri IV, and people could look forward to peace after the long religious wars.

As part of Essex's incursion into high policy, he had taken up Antonio Perez, who lent himself to Philip's enemies in both France and England.[6] But his nuisance-value decreased – as with other traitors in our time – while he hung on and on, outstaying his welcome. Everybody got bored with him, his high-falutin' language and his pretensions – even his patrons in the Essex circle. Essex jokingly 'provided him here of the same office those eunuchs have in Turkey, which is to have the custody of the fairest dames'. The joke was that he was a homosexual (as were both Bacons). Everybody laughed at him.

In May 1595 Perez wrote to Essex a letter 'in that affected style observable in those of his printed among his works, and generally casting an obscurity over the subject upon which he writes'. In his inflated Latin the displeasure of the Queen is that of Juno, while Essex is Hercules, 'clavam potius, tu enim Hercules, Vale clavipotens a clavo impotenti'.[7] Before his departure Perez asked Anthony Bacon for an assurance that Essex loved him; and in taking leave – at last – in June, he would rather die than leave him, 'namque vivendo semper morior, et moriendo semper vivo'.[8] Note the rhetorical flourish. One hears Anthony Bacon's sigh of relief: 'Well, at the last he is gone . . . without my watchfulness and painful patience he would have chanced upon some plot, whereby to have made an aftergame.' Robert

Cecil said the same of him, and Elizabeth couldn't bear him.

In December 1595 Sir George Carey took it very unkindly that the Earl of Pembroke broke off the match intended between his son, Lord Herbert, and Carey's daugher. He told the Queen that it was because Carey would not assure him £1000 a year which comes to his daughter as next heir to Queen Anne Boleyn. However, he has now concluded a match between his daughter and the son and heir of Lord Berkeley, a much older family. It was said at Court that, if Lord Pembroke dies – who was ill – 'the tribe of Hunsdon do lay wait for the wardship of the brave young Lord'. For the young Herbert was under age, only fifteen; it would be some years yet before he would display his heterosexual prowess in seducing Mary Fitton – a contrast with the ambivalent Southampton, seven years his senior and not even yet married.

As we see, these years were busier than ever with multifarious activities, and the Lord Chamberlain was responsible for plays at Court. After the confusion, and suffering of the plague years – two years of plague in succession were abnormal and put a stop to playing in London for most of the time – a new start was to be made, and appropriately under the Lord Chamberlain. The initiative came from the Burbages – James, who was 'Hunsdon's man', and his sons Cuthbert and Richard, who was to become the star actor of the new company. To them they recruited the actor who was, exceptionally, also a writer of plays, William Shakespeare, who had already won success, and Robert Greene's jealousy, with his *Henry VI* plays. He brought with him not only his talents and his considerable business acumen, but the plays already written, *Titus Andronicus, The Comedy of Errors* and possibly a version of *The Taming of the Shrew*.

We are not informed about the other actors who joined in the new combination, but it is thought that Will Kemp the comedian, Thomas Pope, Augustine Phillips, John Heming and Will Sly were in the company from the first. Henry Condell came in later; the most important change was when Will Kemp left in

1599 and his place was taken by Robert Armin, for this was reflected in the parts written for him by the Company's chief dramatist. Richard Burbage was the leading actor who became famous early in the part of Richard III – so much so that stories were told of him as Richard. Many years later, when he died – three years after his life-long colleague, Shakespeare – the Earl of Pembroke wrote shortly after of a gathering of grandees at a play, 'which I, being tender-hearted, could not endure to see so soon after the loss of my old acquaintance, Burbage'. The relationship between Shakespeare and his young patron, Southampton, was even more 'tender-hearted'.

The leading half-dozen actors were sharers in the Lord Chamberlain's Company, i.e. they shared in the profits, along with the Burbages. They were known as fellows, much like the Fellows of a college, who also share in the profits. Trailing along behind them were the other actors, hired men and boys, the servants of the Company. The privileged position of the 'fellows' gave them incentive, and what was remarkable about this Company was its stability, the way the leading men (except Kemp) worked together for the rest of their lives. This shortly made them the leading Company, with a marked ascendancy in performances at Court. When Hunsdon's son, the 2nd Lord Chamberlain Hunsdon, died in 1603 James I took the opportunity to take the premier company under his wing as the King's Men.

We may follow their activities for a while, briefly, in so far as they have left traces in the records. In June 1594 they played with the Admiral's men, performing *Titus Andronicus*, which proved popular, an earlier *Hamlet* and a version of *The Shrew*. In September they were at Marlborough. In October the Lord Chamberlain wrote to the Lord Mayor asking that 'my now Company', i.e. his present company, might continue their occupation of the Crossed Keys inn, their playing-place in the City. At once the Lord Chamberlain's Company took the lead in performances at Court – giving its dramatist a privileged view of what went on there. In March 1595 Richard Burbage, Shakespeare and Kemp received payment for two plays performed at Christmas at Court; in those same Christmas holidays, which lasted until Twelfth Night, they plaed *The Comedy of Errors* at Gray's Inn. On 9 December previously, Hunsdon's son-in-law, Sir Edward Hoby, invited Sir Robert Cecil to his house in Canon Row, Westminster, for a performance: 'where, as late as shall please you, a gate for your supper shall be open, and King Richard present himself to your view'.[9] The busy little statesman – who was sometimes seen in the Presence Chamber coming from the Queen, pre-occupied and his hands full of papers – minuted 'Readily.'

During this period the Chamberlain's Men performed at Court more than all other companies together: on 26, 27, 28 December 1595, and 6 January 1596 – i.e. during Christmas – and on 22 February, at Shrovetide. In February 1596 James Burbage purchased part of the mansion in Blackfriars, next to the properties of Hunsdon and his son, which had been and was to become again a theatre. In July the old Lord Chamberlain died. At once the Lord Mayor and Corporation expelled the players from the City inns. We see what a good friend Hunsdon had been to the players; the Chamberlain's Men were now so securely founded, and worked together so well, that they never looked back.

We may return to the affairs of the family. Simon Forman, who was well acquainted with so many people's private affairs in Elizabethan London, had dealings with several of the Lord Chamberlain's family. In December 1587, when Forman was living in Salisbury, he visited Sir George Carey, Governor of the Isle of Wight. Some years later a question was put to Forman on Carey's behalf, along with Sir Thomas Gorges and the merchant Mr Hawes, whether they will 'obtain stock for a case of things of certain merchandise'. This was a request for an horoscope to be cast, as was regular and frequent with Elizabethans. The *Swallow*, for example, had gone a-roving in the West Indies for Carey in 1591.

In 1601 we find Carey's sister Lady Hoby consulting him medically: she had gout in her hands and feet, swellings in her joints.[10] She was only thirty-four, but the disease had been long upon her, and she was an invalid. Indeed, she had produced an only daughter, no son to inherit the title. This may not have been the only reason, for George Carey, 2nd Lord Hunsdon, had venereal disease. He was dangerously ill and, in May, Lady Hoby came to Forman again to know whether 'the Lord Chamberlain will live or die'. He went down to Bath for the treatment, as people did: it availed him nothing: he died in 1603.

So that it need be no surprise that there turned up among Forman's clients, in the year after the old Lord Chamberlain's death, the young woman who had been his last mistress. This was Emilia Bassano, orphaned daughter of one of the Queen's Italian musicians, Baptist Bassano, who had been brought up in her youth by Susan Bertie, Countess of Kent. From the dedications to him of a number of musical compositions we may assume Hunsdon's interest in music, and we know his keenness for women. He kept this Italianate young women in style, until she proved pregnant, when she was married off in October 1592, with a dowry, to another of the Queen's musicians, Alphonso Lanier.[11]

On 19 March 1594 Lord Burghley noted in his Diary that the Queen went to Somerset House to see the Lord Chamberlain; while on 14 July Essex, Lord Admiral Howard and Hunsdon were at Burghley's house. Both the Lord Chamberlain and the Vice-Chamberlain were sick of the gout in October 1595; Heneage died in November, but Hunsdon recovered. In December we find him and Lord Admiral Howard together at the Tower to view the stores, with special attention to the munitions and arms for next year's campaign. In July 1596 Hunsdon was deperately ill; a daughter-in-law writing to Sir Robert Cecil said that there was no hope for him, and entreated favour for her husband, who hoped for his establishment at Berwick – her Majesty always showed him favours and good thoughts. This is likely to be the second son, John, for we know that Sir George, the heir, did not want his father's office at Berwick, 'where I would be as loth to live as to make a benefit of it by my absence'. He wanted to be Captain of Pensioners, to be near her Majesty's person – the source of all good things.

The old Lord was too sick to make a will, as we find from a nuncupative memorandum, which describes the death-bed scene.[12] On 21 July 1596, after supper, the old man called son George not to leave him that night but to watch with him. Between midnight and 1 a.m. he called him by name: 'as you are mine heir and to possess all and whatsoever I shall leave behind me, so I do think you worthy of it and much more, for I have always found you a kind and loving son'. He wished George to take the administration of all, 'because your mother knoweth not how to deal in such causes so well as yourself, and that I would not have her troubled with so broken and hard estate as I shall leave'. He asked his son to look after her, 'I being able to leave her nothing in respect of that which so good a wife to me and mother to you hath deserved.'

'So also I must leave to your care such of my poor servants as have served me long and I have been able to do nothing for. Her Majesty hath sent me sundry gracious promises on the word of a Prince that she would fully relieve my estate, which, if I shall not live to enjoy, she will confer it upon mine. And therefore doubt not but she will bestow mine offices upon you. . . . So having declared to you my mind and resolution for worldly matters, my mind is satisfied, which hath long been troubled. And now I desire not longer to live and will trouble myself not further with worldly causes. And so I commend myself to God's mercy; and pray for me, good George, and the rest.'

Thus the good, honest old man died.

At once there began the usual clamour for pickings, offices, appointments on a grandee's death. Before he was in his grave Lady Hoby was writing to Cecil of her brother Robert's despair at her Majesty's displeasure: his deputy Wardenship under his father had now gone, while brother John had the occupation of Norham by her Majesty's command – 'she that is nothing but grief and misery, Margaret Hoby'. Simultaneously Sir Edward Stanley was after the keepership of Norham. Lady Hunsdon wanted a favourable grant for her sister in Cornwall, Mrs Trevanion, regarding the salting and packing of fish, i.e. the monopoly of the export of pilchards. She solicited Cecil's help for what would be some small benefit to a poor widow. Actually the Queen treated the ladies quite generously: she made an outright gift of £400 to the widow and two of her daughters and £800 towards the expenses of Hunsdon's grand funeral. In December Lady Hunsdon was provided with the keepership of Somerset House, with its fees, and shortly was awarded an annuity of £200 for life.

Then there followed all the fuss and expense of the funeral of a grandee, a matter of honour since it was that of the Queen's first cousin. Scores of yards of cloth were provided for the Lord Keeper, Lord Treasurer Burghley, the new Lord Chamberlain, Lords Buckhurst, Rich and De la Warr – the Chief Mourner received eight yards at 23s. 4d. a yard; he was attended by six servants with 1½ yards each. The Garter King-at-arms was paid £100 for the hearse, banners, standards – standard-bearers of the late Lord Chamberlain attended by their servants. Knights, gentlemen, doctors of divinity and many others followed in the procession to Westminster Abbey – service of the church costing £20, bays hung round it, £8. 16s. 3d., the dole to the poor, £14. Altogether the grand funeral cost £1106. 17s. The bill was mostly footed by the Queen. So also was that for the huge monument eventually erected – costing some £600 – in St John the Baptist chapel in the Abbey.

The new Lord Hunsdon did not succeed, as he hoped, to his father's office as Lord Chamberlain: it was given to Lord Cobham. Cobham was Cecil's father-in-law, but, we learn, was appointed 'by her Majesty's own choice and care of him'. This group at Court were hostile to Essex and his following; in March 1597 we hear 'how disdainfully my Lord of Essex speaks of him [Cobham] in public. Cobham does likewise protest to hate the Earl as much. What will grow of this I will export.' Thus Rowland Whyte to Sir Robert Sidney in the Netherlands. One thing that grew of it was the Cobhams' strong objection to an earlier member of their family being brought on the stage as Falstaff, by the dramatist of the Essex–Southampton circle. In the two parts of *Henry IV* which he was writing in these years 1597–8, Falstaff was originally called Sir John Oldcastle; at the end of the Second Part Shakespeare had to insert a specific disclaimer: 'for Oldcastle died a martyr, and this is not the man'. At Court the feud continued between the two factions, and once more Southampton's dramatist offended the Cobhams with that figure of fun Master Ford, disguising himself at the Garter Inn as Master Brooke. This was the Cobham family name – Shakespeare had to change it to Broome.

We see how closely linked his work was with the Court, and the denizens of it – not merely in the matter of numerous performances there, nor only in these plays.

The new Lord Hunsdon did not cease to urge his claims upon Cecil and the Queen. He had been barely left by his father, who had 'many more hundreds by office than he hath left scores in land'; this was deplorable considering 'the nearness of my blood'. He proceeded to tot up a schedule of his father's offices, which had brought him in £2147. 3s. 4d. a year; while his landed estate (which nevertheless he owed to the Queen) was worth only £366 a year. He hoped that 'her Majesty, in her love to him who was more careful to serve her than to provide for his, will be mindful of that house which is so near unto her'. So his father had clearly lived right up to his income and beyond it, and had had to sell land. A further demand follows, 'our house so near in blood to hers and so little advanced in her reign of so many years'. There was something in this, for the Careys had long wanted their uncle Boleyn's earldom of Ormonde. Might the new Lord have his father's office of Chief Justice of the Forests?

In March 1597 Lord Cobham conveniently died, and Hunsdon's chance came. In April, 'Lord Hunsdon waits [i.e. on the Queen] and does all things appertaining to the place, but has not yet the white staff.' In a few days, on Sunday 17 April, 'my Lord Hunsdon had the white staff given him, and thereby Lord Chamberlain. The lords being in Council, the Queen sent him to them, where he was sworn Councillor and signed many letters that day.' He had a very shaky signature, from his palsy.

We oberve in all this Elizabeth's essential justice and wisdom regarding her mother's kin. She did not spoil them or treat them with favouritism, frittering away the lands of the Crown upon them; the Careys got far more out of the improvident

James I than they got out of their cousin, for all their constant reminders of 'nearness of blood'. She expected service out of them, and then rewarded them with offices. For all that Sussex used to say of the Careys – that 'they were of the tribe of Dan and were *Noli me tangere*s, implying that they were not to be contested with' – she certainly got good service out of honest and soldierly old Hunsdon.

Sir Robert Naunton in the next generation gives a just estimate of him.[13] 'He was a fast man to his Prince, and firm to his friends and servants. Though he might speak big and therein would be borne out, yet was he not the more dreadful but less harmful, for he was downright. I have heard those that both knew him well, and had interest in him, say merrily of him that his Latin and his dissimulation were both alike. His custom of swearing and obscenity in speaking made him seem a worse Christian than he was, and a better Knight of the Carpet[14] than he should be. As he lived in a ruffling time, so he loved sword and buckler men, and such as our fathers were wont to call men of their hands. Of which sort he had many brave gentlemen that followed him – yet not taken for a popular and dangerous person.' That means – unlike Essex. To sum up: 'this is one that stood amongst the *Togati* [Councillors], of an honest and stout heart, and such a one as would have fought for his Prince and his country; for he had the charge of the Queen's person, both in the Court and the Camp at Tilbury [i.e. at the time of the Armada]'.

We may conclude with this tribute, as from his career, that this honest and soldierly person was a good servant of Queen and country.

SOURCES　Apart from specific references in the notes the main sources are: *Calendars of State Papers, Domestic, Foreign, Scottish,* and *Spanish; The Letters and Papers of Henry VIII; Historical MSS Commission, Salisbury, De L'Isle, Rutland* and *Bath MSS; Sidney Papers,* ed. A. Collins; *Memoirs of the Reign of Queen Elizabeth,* ed. T. Birch; *Illustrations of British History,* ed. E. Lodge; *The Loseley Manuscripts,* ed. A. J. Kempe; *Letters of Philip Gawdy,* ed.

I. H. Jeayes; E. K. Chambers, *The Elizabethan Stage*, II; C. C. Stopes, *Burbage and Shakespeare's Stage*; A. L. Rowse, *Simon Forman: Sex and Society in Shakespeare's Age*; *Desiderata Curiosa*, ed. F. Peck, 2 vols.

Notes

CHAPTER 1   BESS OF HARDWICK: BUILDER AND DYNAST

1. Elizabethans pronounced this 'Barley', as Marlowe was pronounced 'Marley'.
2. V. my *Simon Forman: Sex and Society in Shakespeare's Age*, pp. 32, 48, 279.
3. V. my *The Tower of London*, pp. 99–100.
4. Cf. my edition of *The Poems of Shakespeare's Dark Lady*, p. 52.
5. Cf. my *The Elizabethan Renaissance: The Cultural Achievement*, ch. IV.
6. For him v. my *The Byrons and Trevanions*, pp. 34–8.
7. For William Clowes (pronounced 'Cluse') v. my *The Elizabethan Renaissance: The Cultural Achievement*, pp. 272–6.
8. Concealed lands meant lands, usually monastic or chantry, which should have come to the Crown by the Dissolution, but which had somehow been concealed and withheld.

CHAPTER 2   FATHER PARSONS THE JESUIT
1. Cf. my *Ralegh and the Throckmortons*, pp. 101–2.
2. John Hayward, *An Answer to the First Part of a Certain Conference concerning Succession* (1603).
3. *Historical MSS Commission, Salisbury MSS*, IX, pp. 200, 202–3.
4. Cf. J. W. Allen, *English Political Thought, 1603–1660*, I, pp. 153–4.
5. Edition of 1610.
6. *Recusant Documents from the Ellesmere Manuscripts*, ed. A. G. Petti, Catholic Record Society, vol. 60, pp. 196–7.

CHAPTER 3   EDWARD DE VERE, 17TH EARL OF OXFORD
1. Henry was regularly pronounced Harry in earlier centuries.
2. V. above, p. 48.
3. Cf. my *The Elizabethan Renaissance: The Life of the Society*, p. 160.
4. Cf. my *Shakespeare's Southampton: Patron of Virginia*, pp. 53ff.

CHAPTER 4   ELIZABETH I'S GODSON: SIR JOHN HARINGTON
1. 'Will' had a secondary suggestive meaning in Elizabethan English, as in Shakespeare's Sonnets.

2. Cf. my *Shakespeare's Southampton: Patron of Virginia*, pp. 148ff.
3. Davison had forwarded Elizabeth's warrant for Mary's execution.
4. For him v. my *Ralegh and the Throckmortons*, p. 211.
5. Cf. my *Ralegh and the Throckmortons*, ch. XIII.
6. C. H. Herford and P. Simpson, *Ben Jonson*, II, p. 71.
7. In *The Letters and Epigrams of Sir John Harington*, ed. N. E. McClure (1930).

CHAPTER 5   LORD CHAMBERLAIN HUNSDON
1. *Victoria County History: Hertfordshire*, III, pp. 324ff.
2. Cf. my *The Expansion of Elizabethan England*, pp. 30–1.
3. *Notes and Queries*, 3rd series, VI, pp. 174, 217, 312–13.
4. William Ingram, *A London Life in the Brazen Age: Francis Langley, 1548–1602*, pp. 74–6.
5. He had betrayed Deventer to the Spaniards.
6. For Perez's activities in England in much detail v. G. Ungerer, *A Spaniard in Elizabethan England: The Correspondence of Antonio Perez's Exile*, 2 vols.
7. Impossible to translate Perez's nonsense literally, perhaps we may render it: 'more powerful than the club of Hercules – for you indeed are he – farewell powerful staff from a powerless one'.
8. 'For in living I yet die, and dying I yet live.'
9. Cf. E. K. Chambers, *The Elizabethan Stage*, II, p. 194. Chambers assumes that this refers to *Richard II;* but there is nothing to show whether it might not refer to *Richard III*.
10. Cf. my *Simon Forman: Sex and Society in Shakespeare's Age*, pp. 233–5.
11. For her career v. my Introduction to *The Poems of Shakespeare's Dark Lady*.
12. Somerset House, Prob./11/88, f. 54.
13. Sir Robert Naunton, *Fragmenta Regalia*; Arber's *English Reprints*, pp. 46–7.
14. The *Oxford English Dictionary* cites this phrase but does not give us its meaning. We derive some indication from the title of Robert Greene's *Card of Fancy* (1584), 'wherein the folly of those Carpet Knights is deciphered, which, guiding their course by the compass of Cupid, either dash their ship against most dangerous rocks, or else attain the haven with pain and peril'. It would appear thus to refer to Hunsdon's amorous propensities.

Index